Cycles and Motorcycles

Written by Michael Worthington-Williams
Designed by David Nash
Illustrated by Max Ansell, Mike Atkinson, Richard Hook

First published in this edition 1976
© 1976 William Collins Sons and Company Limited
Published by William Collins Sons and Company Limited
Printed in Great Britain

ISBN 0 00 106242 5

Contents

Collins Transport Series
Cycles and Motorcycles

Collins

Glasgow and London

1 Pedals to Push

was ahead of his time, and it was not until the eighteenth century that we begin to find serious attempts to produce a light road vehicle propelled by muscular effort.

One four-wheeled design of this period—of heavy wooden construction—carried the passenger in a sort of armchair at the front. A servant laboured at the back with a system of cranks and pedals, rather like those on an old-fashioned knife-grinder's cart, being pushed up and down, rather than round and round. In October 1769, a certain Mr. Fergusson was describing a similarly cumbersome, but newly-invented, machine to Dr. Johnson. In this the

Who made the first bicycle? It is a question which may never be answered. We do know that even when the first bicycle was introduced the idea was by no means new. The principle of a mechanical carriage propelled by the person travelling in or upon it can be traced back to Leonardo da Vinci in the fifteenth century. True, his design for a four-wheeler, driven by a bevel gear from a crankshaft, had no steering gear and, as represented, the gearing would have turned the axles in opposite directions! Nevertheless, it was intended that the vehicle should be propelled by the four men it carried. In practical terms, however, Leonardo

Ladies' draisienne, *or hobby-horse, 1819.*

Baron von Drais on his hobby-horse, 1816.

passenger turned a handle which drove a spring which in turn drove the contraption forward. Johnson was not impressed, and remarked 'Then, Sir, what is gained is, the man has the choice whether he will move himself alone or himself and the machine too?' This is really what bicycling is all about.

Kirkpatrick Macmillan, a Scot from Courthill in Dumfriesshire, is usually given credit for the first true bicycle. About 1840 he built a machine driven by treadles which operated the rear wheel. As so often happens with new inventions, the machine made very little impression and only one original was built, although a number of copies were made, those of Thomas McCall and Gavin Dalzell being the best known. Macmillan's machine no longer exists, although the oldest surviving pedal cycle in the world, built by Dalzell in 1845, can be seen in the Museum of Transport in Glasgow.

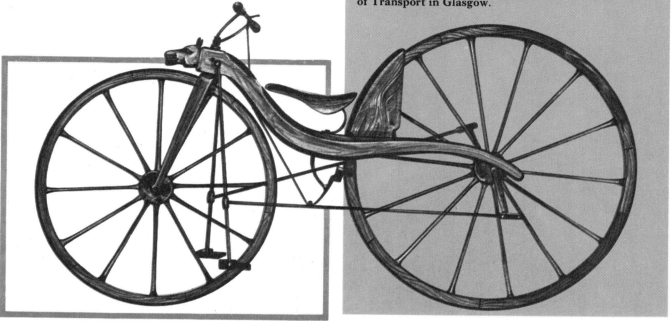

After these early and quite promising beginnings, nothing very much happened. The Russians claim that the bicycle was invented in 1801 by a serf named Artamonov from the Ural Mountains, but it is generally accepted that the *draisienne* or hobby-horse introduced by the German engineer Baron von Drais in 1816 was the father of the modern bicycle. Made of wood, and with iron tyres, the hobby-horse was a simple machine consisting of a wooden cross-bar upon which the rider sat astride on a crude saddle. The bar was supported at front and back by two wheels, the one in front capable of being steered—just. There were no pedals, cranks or brakes, and the rider propelled himself by pushing first one foot and then the other upon the ground in an exaggerated 'walking' motion. Once sufficient momentum had been achieved both feet could be lifted from the ground for a short distance. Downhill runs must have been a hair-raising experience on the cobbled streets of the period.

Over the succeeding 40 years or so there were several more attempts to 'invent' the bicycle. About 1853, Philip Fischer, a German school teacher, built himself a remarkably advanced machine on which to ride to work. Not only did it have a hand-applied brake and luggage box, but also

a warning bell activated by a device which could be turned into the spokes. In 1862, a man named Karl Kech added cranks and pedals to an early hobby-horse which worked directly on the hub of the front wheel, but this was a very crude machine and was soon forgotten.

France takes the honours for popularizing the bicycle. Pierre Michaux, a Parisian maker of perambulators, was the man who really launched them in 1861. His machines, like Kech's, were at first simply adaptations of the earlier hobby-horse, pedals and cranks being added. But in only six years they evolved into graceful velocipedes with such luxuries as pneumatic saddles, grease cups, back-rests and ivory handle grips. Instead of the heavy wooden construction of the earlier machines, damascened steel was used. This made them lighter and stronger than their predecessors and led to some degree of standardization.

Britain did not start to produce bicycles until 1869, and then it was only an accident that things happened as they did. The Coventry Sewing Machine Company had been persuaded by their Paris agent Rowley B. Turner to manufacture 400 bicycles for the French market. When the outbreak of the Franco–Prussian War prevented the shipping of the machines to France, they were sold in

7

England. With front-wheel drive, they immediately became popular, and progress in Britain thereafter matched that in France.

The cycle pioneer James Starley started his career with the Coventry Sewing Machine Company and as a result of the order for bicycles from France became greatly interested in the new industry. With William Hillman, he set up a business to manufacture Ariel cycles. Initially these were lightweight, all-metal ordinaries, or penny-farthings, as they later became known.

Because of the unstable nature of the ordinary, bicycling was anything but dull and the new sport attracted to its ranks a breed of athletic and adventurous young men who quickly formed themselves into clubs. Poorer people could

serious. The nineteenth century had witnessed the birth and tremendous expansion of the railways. The success of this new means of transport led to a decline in road maintenance, and the cycle clubs were quick to complain.

The clubs were also concerned with road safety, a subject almost universally ignored until that time. While having to suffer the indignity of being called 'ironmongery riders' and 'cads on castors', in 1888 bicyclists were successful in having a law passed in Britain which made it compulsory for all vehicles to carry lights at night, even though the same law made it necessary for cyclists to carry a bell which had to ring all the time the machine was in motion.

When James Starley died in 1881, his nephew John carried on his work, having already set up in business in

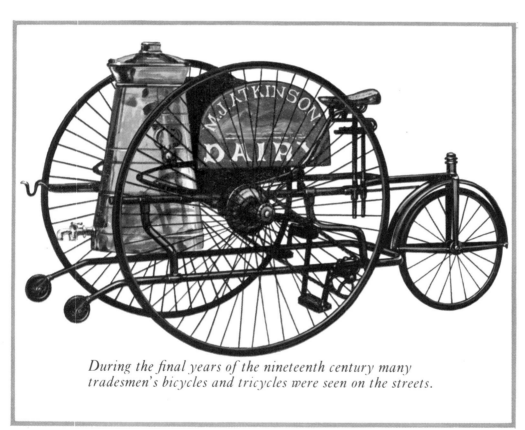

During the final years of the nineteenth century many tradesmen's bicycles and tricycles were seen on the streets.

American convertible tricycle of the 1870s.

Tricycle with direct drive to front wheels.

not afford the relatively high purchase price of the machines then available and since the gentry considered the bicycle beneath their dignity, club members were largely affluent and middle class.

Anyone who has taken a 'header' from a modern machine can appreciate the hazards which faced the rider who attempted to negotiate pot-hole after pot-hole from the lofty insecurity of an ordinary, with his feet engaged in both pedalling and steering. The more cycles there were, the more accidents that occurred, and these were often

1877 with William Sutton at the Meteor Works in Coventry to build some of his uncle's designs in his own right. His Meteor tricycle earned much favourable comment in the cycle press of the day. It was John who first named one of his models the Rover, and the motor cars which bear the same name today are direct descendants of that machine.

Manufacturers realized that it would take time to improve the roads and tried hard to produce safer bicycles. In 1879 Rudge (later famous for motorcycles) became the first firm to introduce a chain-driven machine which sold in

Ernest Michaux in 1868.

John Starley on his Rover safety bicycle in 1885. Starley's machine set the pattern for the future development of the cycle and after its introduction the days of the ordinary and the tricycle were numbered.

The first Rover bicycle, built in 1884, suffered from indirect steering. An improved model, introduced in 1885, achieved instant popular acclaim, and in it the shape of the modern cycle can clearly be seen. In the same year the ordinary reached its peak of popularity, but from then onwards its devotees fought a rearguard action against overwhelming odds. At one time it had looked as if the tricycle would replace the ordinary in the sales race—between 1886 and 1888 there were still more three-wheelers at the annual shows than two-wheelers—but in 1888 John Boyd Dunlop introduced a device which, allied to the Rover, was to set the pattern of bicycle development for the next 60 or 70 years.

This device was Dunlop's pneumatic rubber tyre. Until 1889, despite the adoption of sprung saddles and smaller wheels, cyclists still experienced a pretty rough ride on their solid rubber tyres. To counter this, a number of models with sprung frames made their appearance, but these were only partly successful in mitigating the agony. The pneumatic tyre was not new, of course. It was first patented by another Scotsman, Robert Thomson, as early as 1845. At that time, however, technology and materials were not sufficiently advanced to take full advantage of the invention, and it was soon forgotten. What Dunlop did was to make the pneumatic tyre a practicable proposition.

By 1892, solid-tyred machines simply would not sell, and to survive, manufacturers had to redesign their frames and wheels to accept Dunlop's tyres. Of course, punctures were a problem and a cushion tyre was one of several attempts to overcome this. But such was the boom

Cycling club on ordinaries in the 1880s.

reasonable numbers. It bore a resemblance to the modern bicycle, but for some reason did not 'catch on' and after being dubbed 'the crocodile' by an unappreciative public, it was dropped. Another design was the Kangaroo, a chain-driven ordinary with the pedals offset from the hub of the front wheel, which was considerably smaller than that on standard ordinaries. During these early days of chain drive, however, the chains tended to stretch after a period of use. This caused backlash, which made the system unpopular until it was improved.

in bicycles between 1890 and 1900 that Dunlop found himself with adequate finance and was able constantly to improve his production methods. This reduced the number of punctures in his products to an acceptable level.

Fitted with pneumatic tyres, bicycles at last became acceptable transport for women. By 1895 the well-to-do had also decided that cycling could be fashionable and respectable. Like most fashions, however, it declined, and by 1900 the motor car was beginning, noisily and uncertainly, to make its presence felt on the roads of the world.

2 Early Motor Cycles

Nicholas Cugnot's steam tricycles of 1765 are generally considered to be the first self-propelled vehicles. Various other machines made their appearance in the late eighteenth and early nineteenth centuries, but the only one which could remotely be considered as a motorcycle turned out to be a hoax. Rejoicing in the name *Vélocipèdraisiavaporianna* (steam-driven velocipede), which, as was intended, suggested that the machine was a steam-powered hobby-horse or draisienne, it was reported together with a celebrated illustration that this remarkable machine had given a demonstration in the Luxembourg Gardens in Paris on 5 April 1818. In fact, it had done nothing of the sort, being no more than the product of an artist's imagination. Nevertheless, like many unintentional prophesies, some of its features were later to be incorporated in actual machines.

This amusing report did not at the time inspire inventors to try to produce such a machine and almost 50 years passed before authentic designs emerged. Once again, France was to the fore, Pierre Michaux claiming some of the credit when he fitted a light steam engine to one of his velocipedes in 1867. Who designed the engine is not known, but a year later a M. Perreaux took out a patent for a steam motorcycle using a Michaux machine. Belt-driven to the rear wheel from a single-cylinder engine, the Michaux-Perreaux enjoyed the doubtful advantage of a petroleum burner mounted immediately below the saddle.

Meanwhile in the United States, at Roxbury, Massachusetts, Sylvester Howard Roper—who had been experimenting with steam transport for ten years before the velocipede became popular—fitted a number of heavy wooden-wheeled vehicles with single-cyclinder steam engines and enormous boilers in the 1860s. During the same period he became associated with a showman named 'Professor' W.W. Austen, who is often credited with having built steam vehicles himself. These were, in fact, Roper's designs although the 'Professor', who made his living

demonstrating them at circuses and country fairs, was not above claiming the credit for himself. Roper was killed at the Charles River cycle track in Boston in 1896, after having been thrown from a motorcycle. Thus he met the same fate as his friend Austen who, two years earlier, had been killed when his machine collided with another steam vehicle—possibly the first two-car crash in the world.

The next significant development, following the first Ropers, was another American design built in Phoenix, Arizona by Lucius D. Copeland. Another American, Colonel A.A. Pope, a pioneer of the cycle industry, was firmly established by 1881 building Columbia high-wheeled bicycles at his plant at Hartford, Connecticut, and Copeland chose a Columbia machine in which to install his first lightweight 0·25-h.p. steam engine. This proved unsuitable, and Copeland's next choice was a machine called the Star. This was similar to an ordinary, except that the 'farthing' wheel was in the front rather than at the rear, and for this reason proved more successful. After obtaining financial backing from Sanford Northrup of Camden, New Jersey, Copeland formed a company and is said to have built some 200 'motocycles' before deciding that there was insufficient profit to be made. Capable of between nineteen and twenty-four kilometres (twelve and fifteen miles) per hour, they seem to have been remarkably reliable, and a tricycle was taken on a 192-kilometre (120-mile) trip to Atlantic City and back without apparent trouble, but by 1890 Copeland had abandoned his efforts.

Over the years, a great deal of publicity has been given to the motorcycle which Gottlieb Daimler produced in 1885, but its real significance is that it was powered by the first high-speed four-stroke internal combustion engine. It was never intended that it should be built in large numbers for sale, and indeed with its cumbersome wooden frame, outriggers and iron tyres, it is unlikely that it would have tempted many buyers. It did however prove a valuable testing apparatus for Daimler's engine, which was eventually developed for use in the motor car.

It has often been said that 'you can't get something for nothing' and the machine devised by a Mr. Brownhill of Staffordshire in England in the early 1880s is a good example

The Cynophère, illustrated on the opposite page, was invented in France and patented in the United States in 1875. It consisted of two large wheels between which was a comfortable seat and footrest. The guide wheel in front was controlled by a rod to the driver's right hand. At his left hand was a brake to regulate the speed. Power was furnished by two dogs, each running on a treadway within the side wheels. Advertisements of the day claimed that so light was the vehicle that it was no more exertion for the dogs to run upon the treadways of the wheels than it was for them to go at the same speed along the highway at their own pleasure.

Lucius D. Copeland and his steam motorcycle of 1885.

(Left, top) Parkyns–Bateman steam motor tricycle, 1881. (Centre) Cynophère, driven by dog-power. (Bottom) Michaux–Perreaux steam motorcycle, 1869.

Drawing based on a contemporary print of the Vélocipèdraisiavaporianna.

of the truth of this statement. Brownhill's idea was that when his vehicle freewheeled downhill, air would be compressed in a reservoir, and that this reserve of compressed power could then be used to propel it uphill and on the level. Although his scheme failed dismally, not all English inventors were so unlucky.

Despite having an engine of most unusual design, Edward Butler's tricycle actually worked. He exhibited the drawings at the 1884 Stanley Cycle Show in London and had a complete vehicle running at the Inventions Exhibition the following year. This boasted such advanced features as electric ignition, chain-driven rotary valves and a carburettor similar in principle to those in use today. Its twin-cylinder horizontal engine transmitted power through connecting rods and cranks direct to the single rear wheel. Steering was by means of two vertical levers on either side of the operator, similar to those on a modern bulldozer.

Lack of money prevented further development, and in the event Britain was plagued at this early date by anti-motoring laws which effectively discouraged any serious attempts at motor car or motorcycle manufacture. The *Locomotives on Highways Act* (1861) limited the speed of mechanical vehicles to 3·2 kilometres (two miles) per hour in towns or 6·4 kilometres (four miles) per hour on the open road and also made it compulsory for a person to walk 55 metres (60 yards) ahead with a red flag (or a red lantern at night). In view of this it is scarcely surprising that the few oil-engined two-stroke machines built in England from 1892 were mainly sold in France.

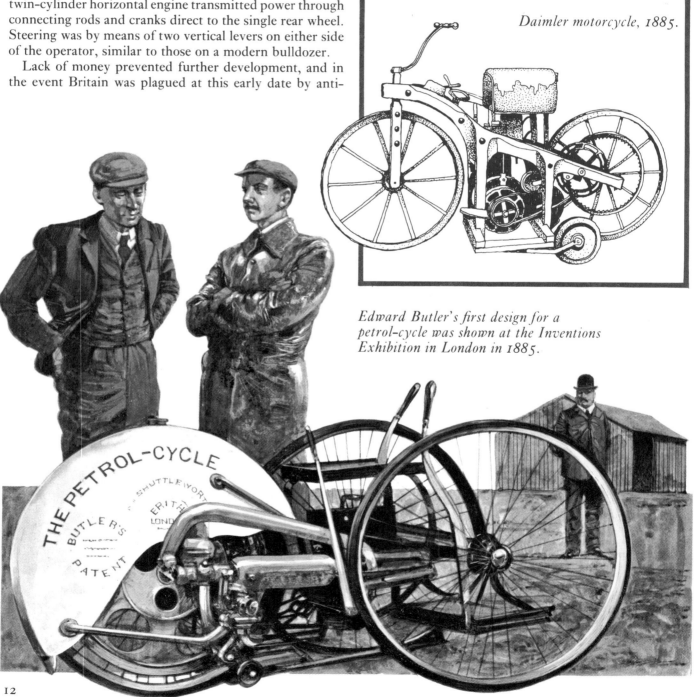

Daimler motorcycle, 1885.

Edward Butler's first design for a petrol-cycle was shown at the Inventions Exhibition in London in 1885.

THE PETROL-CYCLE
BUTLER'S
PATENT
SHUTTLEWORTH
ERITH
LONDON

It was in Munich, Germany that motorcycle production first achieved an output of any size. This was mainly due to the appearance of the Wolfmuller in 1894. It was the first really practical design for a motorcycle and large numbers were built both in Germany and France. A two-cylinder, four-stroke machine, with an engine of about 1·5 litres, it transmitted its power direct to the rear wheel by open connecting rods and cranks. The rods were attached to adjustable points near the cylinder head by rubber bands which, when they contracted after the power

stroke, helped the piston to return to its original position for the compression stroke. Like Daimler's experimental machine, the Wolfmuller employed a surface carburettor and ignition by hot tube. This was a backward step in design following the efforts of Edward Butler, but, nevertheless, 38 kilometres (24 miles) per hour could be achieved. The Wolfmuller was entered in the 1895 Paris–Bordeaux–Paris race but did not put up much of a showing, and by 1897 the company was out of business.

The limelight turned once again upon France. This time it was the turn of the firm of De Dion, Bouton in Paris. Their designs were to have a much more lasting effect upon the motor industry than had those of their predecessors. The company, which had originally concentrated upon steam designs, was formed as De Dion, Bouton and Trépardoux in 1882, and it is hard to imagine more apparently unsuitable partners. The Marquis Albert de Dion was a wealthy aristocrat, whilst brothers-in-law Bouton and Trépardoux were impoverished makers of steam vehicles. After making a number of steam tricycles during the 1880s, the decision was taken to adopt the internal combustion engine. Trépardoux was a confirmed steam enthusiast and in 1894 he resigned in disgust, but this did not prevent the remaining partners from producing their first motor tricycle in 1895. The tiny 0·5-h.p. engine was mounted vertically at the rear, driving the axle through exposed gearing. The petrol relied upon the rough ride which the unsprung tricycle gave it to produce an evaporated and therefore combustible mixture in the crude surface carburettor provided. Nevertheless, engine speeds previously quite unheard of, twice the 900 revolutions per minute of the Daimler, were achieved.

The first commercially successful tricycle was made by James Starley in the 1870s. He was responsible not only for the development of early designs but also for many of the subsequent improvements to them. In 1880 Starley added another large driving wheel to the tricycle, thus converting the machine into a four-wheeler, in which the two riders were seated side by side. The small rear wheel was then discarded and the machine was a tricycle once more, this time with front-wheel steering, which was eventually distributed to both wheels. These improvements led to the Salvo tricycle which acquired the name 'Royal' Salvo because of the patronage and interest of Queen Victoria. Two machines were ordered by the Queen in 1881 while she was staying at Osborne House on the Isle of Wight. James Starley was commanded to appear before her with the machine so that she might learn from the inventor first-hand how they operated. There is no record of the Queen ever mounting the tricycle, but there is no doubt that such royal interest gave great impetus to the tricycle industry.

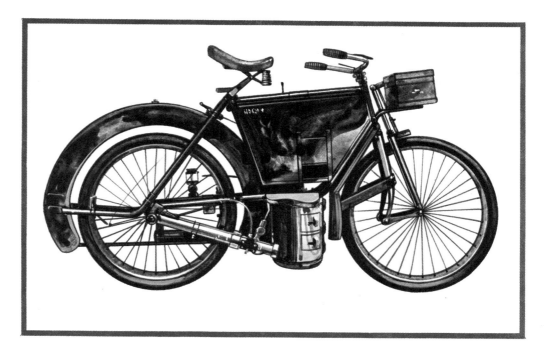

The Dalifol steam motorcycle of 1894 was a French design based on a frame of safety-bicycle form. The steel furnace under the tubular boiler was fed from a hopper with small coke.

By 1899 the De Dion had become extremely popular and was widely copied. In that year one was entered in the Paris–Bordeaux race and despite atrocious roads averaged 45 kilometres (28 miles) per hour over the route, the engine by that time having been enlarged to 2·5-h.p. Because the weight was all at the rear, however, the machine had a

whenever the occasion demanded—which was often.

Motorcyclists as a group tended to be looked down upon by motorists, and could expect little assistance from their fellow-travellers when emergencies arose. In spite of all these setbacks, or perhaps because of them, the motorcyclist became a member of a breed apart. He was tough,

tendency to tip up, and although the design proved the worth of the air-cooled, single-cylinder engine, the tricycle layout did not survive long into the twentieth century.

In Paris, the brothers Michel and Eugene Werner, of French nationality but Russian extraction, had other ideas. They mounted their 0·75-h.p. engine in front of the handlebars where it drove the front wheel by a belt of twisted rawhide. By comparison with the De Dion it was a crude machine. It had to be pedalled up hills and displayed an unhealthy tendency to side-slip, whereupon, having unseated the unhappy rider, a cheerful blaze could be relied upon to finish the job. Nevertheless, with a slight rearrangement of its component parts, the Werner represented much more closely the pattern of development which the motorcycle was to follow in the ensuing years.

Viewing this early period now, it is difficult to see quite how the motorcycle survived into the twentieth century at all. Things were difficult enough for the early owners of motor cars, but at least they had a measure of protection from the elements, could carry an emergency supply of fuel, tools and—most important—spare tyres. But the intrepid motorcyclist was exposed to quagmires of mud, could carry no spares, and such tools as existed were carried in a tool box little larger than a box of household matches. Most motor cars, owned as they were by the wealthy, were driven by paid chauffeurs who were trained in their repair, whereas the motorcyclist had to be his own chauffeur, repairer and mechanic, prepared to 'get off and get under'

resourceful and enthusiastic for his chosen mode of travel, and defended it fiercely against all critics. A strong bond grew up among motorcyclists which lasted long after the similar comradeship of the road shared by drivers of motor cars had evaporated. At the very time when optimism had been replaced by severe doubts as to the practicability of the motorcycle (expressed by the larger manufacturers and the motoring press) the enthusiasm of the riders spurred them to greater efforts.

At this time motor cars were something of a fad indulged in only by the rich, who considered it was fashionable to own one. Motorcycles tended to be avoided by them, if only because it is difficult to look elegant when sprawled in the mud grappling with a tangled heap of scrap iron. But the very fact that the motorcycle was not at this stage a practical and efficient means of travelling from one point to another emphasised its potential as a machine simply for pleasure. Many of the earliest riders were drawn from the ranks of those who had become enthusiastic 'two-wheelers' during the bicycle craze of the early 1890s. This association with motorcycling as a pastime persisted (and does to this day) long after roads, motor cars and motorcycles had been improved to a stage when all were completely reliable. Thus we find that even when motor cars had become cheap enough for all, many motorcyclists clung to two wheels because of the enjoyment and exhilaration which the motorcycle afforded. This fact is important when we come to look at the development which took place after 1900.

The three motorcycles below are, from left to right: Hildebrand and Wolfmuller motorcycle, 1894; 2·5 h.p. Royal Enfield four-wheeler, 1898; and 1·5 h.p. Werner motorcycle, 1899.

Whenever a new industry emerges it attracts to its ranks not only those of inventive genius and vision who are able to contribute to its advancement but also those who see opportunities to get rich quickly. Edward Joel Pennington fell more or less equally into each category. An American, he was born in 1858 in Indiana and at the age of thirteen was apprenticed as a pattern maker. In the 1880s he embarked on a colourful career which was to take him from one end of the United States to the other. In the early nineties he turned his attention to the motor vehicle and in 1895 made his way to England. It is some measure of his persuasive ability that he managed to sell his worthless patents to the astute businessman H.J. Lawson. Even so, it is difficult to imagine what possessed Lawson to hand over £100,000 in cash to Pennington for a machine which invariably failed to run successfully for more than a few minutes at a time, totally lacked a cooling device, was scantily lubricated and managed to do away with the necessity for a carburettor. Lawson's companies, financed from the money he had made from the bicycle industry, collapsed in ruins in 1904. Meanwhile, Pennington, having exhausted his fortune on expensive living, declared himself bankrupt and returned to the United States.

De Dion, Bouton motor tricycle, 1898.

Facts & Figures

ERIC FERNIHOUGH

Eric Fernihough had a long and distinguished career covering virtually the whole of the period between the wars. Commencing with a 250-c.c. side-valve New Imperial, he challenged the 350-c.c. o.h.v. class and made an impressive showing despite the unsuitability of his mount. His successes with the 'Imp' and with his 246-c.c. Excelsior J.A.P. were largely due to his own meticulous preparation of the machines he rode. He graduated in the thirties to the larger Brough Superiors and throughout the decade was consistently successful. As late as 1937 he achieved the impressive speed of 270 kilometres (169·8 miles) per hour in Hungary, capturing the world's solo standing start kilometre record and capped this with the sidecar record of 217·36 kilometres (137·1 miles) per hour. In March 1938 he attained 229·28 kilometres (143·3 miles) per hour.

This freak tandem was appropriately named Eiffel. It was made about 1897 and was probably used as a publicity stunt.

CHAIN DRIVE

Having adopted chain drive for the bicycle in the 1880s, it might have been thought that the manufacturers would have continued to use it on the motorcycle, but this was not so. Many of the early machines had no clutch, being merely pedalled manually until the engine could be induced to fire. Had a chain been fitted the resulting 'snatch' would have broken the chain or stripped the teeth off the sprocket, or at least ripped the spokes out of the driving wheel. Belts made of leather, on the other hand, were less positive in their grip and apt to slip, enabling a smoother take up of the drive.

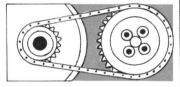

SCOTT ENGINES

Every now and then an unorthodox design emerges which, because of its overall excellence, manages to overcome the prejudices of the buying public and the resultant sales resistance. Such a machine was the Scott. Angus Scott was one of the earliest advocates of the two-stroke engine, but like a great many engineer/inventors he seemed more interested in experimentation and design than in making money. Although his earliest machines were built prior to 1900, it was not until 1908 that commercial production of his parallel twin two-strokes commenced. Early exponents of variable gearing and the kick starter, Scott machines were entered in the 1911 and 1912 T.T. events, winning the latter comfortably to the anguish of competing manufacturers of four-stroke machines. The Scott, with an engine of 487-c.c., had been the smallest of the contenders.

CUDDLERS

A peculiar breed of machine which began to make its appearance in 1913 was the motorcycle taxi. Never really popular, these were motorcycle combinations with large sidecars. Most had large flat-twin engines with either air or water cooling and carried two passengers side by side or, sometimes, two in front and one at the rear of their enormous enclosed cab bodies. They found some favour with operators in seaside resorts where they were treated as something of a novelty and earned themselves the nickname 'cuddlers'.

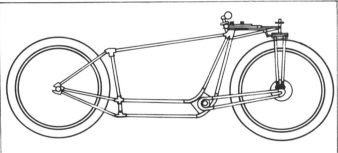

IDLER WHEEL

A feature of some motorcycle designs in the early 1900s was the idler wheel. One was fitted on either side of the rear axle. These could be raised or lowered when stopping or running slowly in heavy traffic. This meant that the rider who felt insecure on two wheels had the reassurance of converting his mount into one of four wheels. As the Peerless

Champion advertisements put it—their motorcycle, with its underslung frame and low centre of gravity, was a car anybody could ride.

GEORGE WALLIS

The hub-steered motorcycle (above) designed by George Wallis in the 1920s was a revolutionary design which led to a machine of great stability. A development of this motorcycle became a standard mount for speedway riders in the 1930s. Wallis was one-time racing manager for Harley-Davidson's British company and throughout his life has been a prolific inventor and designer.

THE SLINGER

The Slinger, introduced in 1903, was perhaps the only articulated motorcycle ever made. Its large single-cylinder engine was mounted in front of the main body of the machine on two small wheels and the rider was towed behind. Thus placed, he was exactly in position to receive a full quota of oil and exhaust fumes, which is probably why Mr. Slinger was out of business by 1904.

HORSMAN AND DIXON

Vic Horsman (above left) was a notable member of that elite breed of pre-war racing motorcyclists—the tuner/riders. Some indication of what could be achieved with a 'tweaked' machine may be gained from the fact that in 1920 he coaxed his side-valve, single-gear, belt-driven Norton to 114·69 kilometres (71·68 miles) per hour. By 1912 his Norton boasted a three-speed gear and chain drive, but shortly afterwards he switched to a Triumph. Combining the qualities of the Ricardo engine with special alcohol fuel and a lowered frame, he broke the 500-c.c. flying start eight-kilometre (five-mile) record at 188·5 kilometres (92·82 miles) per hour. He was equally at home with the larger 599-c.c. Triumph in solo and sidecar events, and also competed with a 490-c.c. Norton, winning the 500-c.c. solo championship. Freddie Dixon (above right) was one of those larger-than-life characters who contributed so much to the atmosphere of Brooklands between the wars. A fearless rider, there was no machine that he could not ride, and his early successes were scored with the big eight-valve 998-c.c. vee-twin Harley-Davidsons. Prominent in both hill climbs and sprints, as well as on the track, he frequently bettered 160 kilometres (100 miles) per hour in the early twenties taking the world's flying start kilometre record on the Bois de Boulogne track at 148 kilometres (106·8 miles) per hour in 1923. At the Arpajon Speed Trials in 1927 he managed 208 kilometres (130 miles) per hour three times on a Brough Superior.

HARRY RICARDO

Harry Ricardo, a born engineer, built a water-pumping engine while still in his teens, and a steam-powered motorcycle while at school. As an undergraduate he designed a two-stroke engine for marine and motor car use. During the war he was concerned with the design of engines for tanks and in 1919 established his own research laboratory. By chance, he acquired a Triumph motorcycle and one of his assistants, Frank Halford, managed some impressive wins at Brooklands on it—after Ricardo had modified certain of its parts. The Triumph company commissioned Ricardo to design a new engine for their machine and the resultant Triumph-Ricardo proved a bestseller for several years.

THE AUTO-GLIDER

The Auto-Glider Motor-Scooter, despite its relatively modern appearance, dates from the year 1915. Powered by a 292-c.c. Villiers two-stroke engine, the makers claimed the machine was capable of 64 kilometres (40 miles) per hour. Two types were made: the style shown where the rider sat down and another on which he stood on a low-level platform.

BROOKLANDS

Brooklands was designed by the same Colonel Holden who had built the 1897 Holden motorcycle and was financed largely by H.F. Locke King who owned the land at Weybridge, Surrey on which it was built. The circuit opened in 1907, about twelve months after construction was commenced. Measuring just under six kilometres (three miles) round its perimeter the banked concrete track was 30·48 metres (100 feet) wide. Largely intended to counteract the ban on road racing and to attract the larger events to Britain, Brooklands had been conceived as a shop window for the motor industry and as such received considerable support from established manufacturers.

3 Belts Clips & Braces

choice awaited the would-be motorcyclist. The only guide to help the prospective buyer were the claims that the respective manufacturers made for their machines.

The alternatives available ranged from 'power trailers', with their own driven wheel which could be clipped on behind an ordinary bicycle, to the Perks and Birch motor-wheel manufactured by Singer and fitted as front-wheel drive to tricycles (some of which had a tandem seat) or as rear-wheel drive to ladies' models. This latter ingenious device housed the engine within the spokes of the wheel and pre-dated the Cyclemaster unit of the 1950s by almost half a century.

Quadricycles, similar to the De Dion but with four wheels, also enjoyed a brief vogue, and at least two—the Cudell and the Simms—were adapted for military use, the latter carrying a Maxim machine-gun. By far the strongest rival of the motor bicycle for sales, however,

(Right) three h.p. Renaux motor tricycle, 1899.

1907 trademark of Rex, the British motor company in Coventry which made motorcycles.

The motorcycle industry grew directly out of the bicycle boom of the 1890s. With the layout of the safety cycle established it would seem natural that manufacturers should have used the standard bicycle frame as the basis for a motorized version. Although the Werner brothers and a few others did just this, opinion was in fact widely divided on what course the development of the motorcycle should take.

The success of the De Dion tricycle, despite its short-comings, was such that at least 50 firms were offering similar designs, and all the indications at the turn of the century were that this type of machine would emerge triumphant. But it was not to be, and a bewildering

was the tricar, or forecar. First introduced by Humber in 1898, at a time when the company was still very much influenced by H.J. Lawson, and designed by E.J. Pennington, the tricar did not immediately become popular. When J. van Hooydonk of Phoenix reintroduced it as the Trimo in 1902, he claimed to be the originator of the design and some heated correspondence with Humber followed in the motoring press. All the same, the Trimo enjoyed a fair degree of popularity for some years until it was dropped in favour of a small car.

Although the original Humber design carried the engine on an outrigger at the rear, most tricars settled for a mid-engine layout driving the single rear wheel by belt.

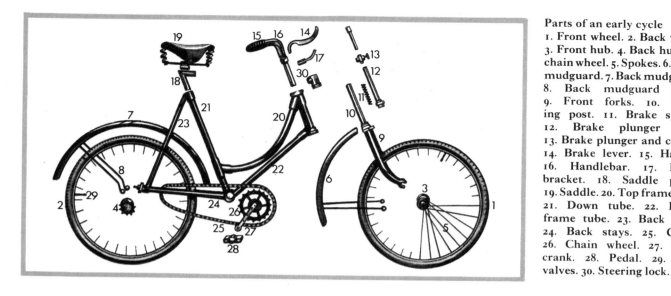

Parts of an early cycle
1. Front wheel. 2. Back wheel. 3. Front hub. 4. Back hub and chain wheel. 5. Spokes. 6. Front mudguard. 7. Back mudguard. 8. Back mudguard stays. 9. Front forks. 10. Steering post. 11. Brake spring. 12. Brake plunger tube. 13. Brake plunger and clamp. 14. Brake lever. 15. Handle. 16. Handlebar. 17. Lamp bracket. 18. Saddle pillar. 19. Saddle. 20. Top frame tube. 21. Down tube. 22. Lower frame tube. 23. Back forks. 24. Back stays. 25. Chain. 26. Chain wheel. 27. Right crank. 28. Pedal. 29. Tyre valves. 30. Steering lock.

The rider sat on a saddle and steered the two front wheels by handlebars. These supported between them a sprung 'chair' of the bath chair variety, often of wickerwork, in which the unhappy passenger almost froze or choked to death on dust, harassed by the knowledge that he was nearest to any accident if and when it occurred.

Another arrangement, potentially even more dangerous than the forecar, had the passenger being carried in a rickshaw-type trailer, towed by a single tie-bar behind a motor bicycle. Quite apart from subjecting the luckless occupant to a constant head-on stream of road dust and exhaust fumes, the tie-bar frequently parted company with the bicycle, depositing the passenger unceremoniously in the road.

The most obvious disadvantage of both the forecar and rickshaw designs was the virtual impossibility of any conversation between driver and passenger. It was perhaps this factor more than any other which encouraged manufacturers to seek other solutions. In Britain Messrs. Mills and Fulford came up with the answer in 1902. They designed a 'sociable' attachment, which consisted of the forecar itself, with one wheel removed, attached alongside the motor bicycle. Thus the modern combination with sidecar was born, although the earliest examples were totally exposed 'chairs' with little or no protection for the occupant. By 1903 several other similar sidecars were on the market, and from that time onward the forecar and tricycle types went into decline.

At first, little attempt was made to design a motorcycle as such, and the first solo machines to appear in any numbers after 1900 were motor bicycles—that is, bicycles with an engine clipped to the frame. The positioning of the engine varied, and whilst the Werners favoured the engine in front of the handlebars, others such as the Princeps, built in Northampton, England, carried it mounted forward, sloping within the 'diamond' of the

The significance of the route from the southernmost point of Britain at Land's End in Cornwall to John o' Groats in north Scotland as a suitable subject for record-breaking attempts has long been recognized. The 'End-to-End', as it was known, had been covered in ordinaries as early as the 1870s, when the 1,280 kilometres (800-mile) journey took about eleven days. The racing cyclist G.P. Mills (seen below) established a new record on an ordinary of just over five days in 1886. Later, in 1893, this time on a Humber tricycle, he reduced the time to three days, five hours, 49 minutes.

Headlamp from an early bicycle.

This bicycle skate was the invention of an American living in New York in 1901.

This giant eight-man tricycle was built in the United States in 1896. Each of the large wheels was three and a half metres (eleven feet) in diameter.

frame and driving the rear wheel by belt. As with most machines, the pedal gear was retained, both for starting and to give pedal assistance on hills. The Princeps was quite advanced for its time, having a 'free' engine and variable gearing. This meant that while other machines had but a single speed and their riders had to stall the engine in order to stop, the engine of the Princeps could be permitted to run while the machine was at rest. The added luxury of a friction clutch enabled the rider to start again without pedalling. The Princeps was a British machine, but most of the early successful 'clip-on' types such as the Minerva 1·75-h.p. originated on the continent of Europe.

In the United States, the pattern of evolution differed. The tricycle and forecar designs never really gained a foothold. On solo machines, a cigar-shaped fuel tank was more often favoured, giving a more streamlined appearance. The Indian, destined to become one of America's most famous motorcycles, followed this pattern. In its earliest forms it looked like a bicycle with the engine stuck on as an afterthought. In this case it was directly under the saddle, which must have been a little uncomfortable for the rider.

In both Europe and the United States, the engine gradually assumed a more central position. The frame was adapted to accommodate it and strengthened where necessary, and because pedalling had now become a secondary consideration, the saddle was lowered to a position behind the fuel tank. The whole profile of machines could therefore be reduced in height and lengthened. As well as improving appearance, this also lowered the centre of gravity and made the machines far more stable and easier to control. Pedals were still retained, especially on the smaller machines, until well after the outbreak of the First World War.

Initially, most engines were air-cooled and single-cylinder of the simplest type. There were some water-cooled examples such as the 2·5-h.p. Iris of 1903, and the Jesmond of the same year, which did enjoy limited popularity. Certainly, some of the larger tricars fitted water-cooled units, mainly because of the difficulty of cooling the engine when it was situated behind the front-mounted passenger.

As yet, most engines were of the four-stroke type, since the two-stroke engine suffered from an inherited prejudice which dated back to the nineteenth-century stationary gas engines which operated on the two-cycle principle. They had been notoriously difficult to start (mainly due to their crude ignition systems) and as a result the two-stroke engine was not popular.

The vee-twin engine appeared quite early on. With the advance in popularity of the sidecar combination, and the increased weight which resulted, the vee-twin became a favoured power unit for this type of machine, for which its balanced power output was admirably suited.

Despite a healthy choice of designs, the motorcycle was still not accepted universally as a practical alternative to the motor car, and it must be admitted that in the more widely-publicized reliability events the results were hardly encouraging. The 1,000 Miles Trial organized in 1900 by the Automobile Club of Great Britain and Ireland (later the Royal Automobile Club) had attracted a few three-wheeled entries but only two of these managed to complete the course. The 1900 event had been intended primarily to demonstrate the reliability of the motor car as a means of transport rather than the flimsier motorcycle, but the R.A.C. formed an Auto Cycle Club (later the Auto Cycle Union) and organized a trial purely for motorcycles. The contestants were to complete 1,600 kilometres (1,000 miles) in all, this to be achieved by ten consecutive daily 160-kilometre (100-mile) excursions. The organization of the trial left a great deal to be desired and the event, which took place in August 1903, was totally boycotted by several manufacturers due to what they felt were unacceptable conditions. The results can hardly be said to be representative, but of 43 starters twenty managed to last the course.

Until the advent of the 1,000 Miles Trial, the accent had been, in the competitive sense, on speed rather than reliability and some remarkable performances had been achieved. Speeds of up to 144 kilometres (80 miles) per hour were set up over relatively short distances and upon prepared surfaces. It is significant that the machines used

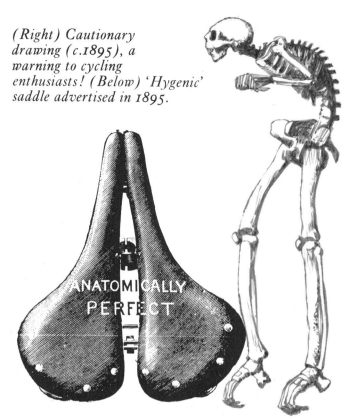

(Right) Cautionary drawing (c.1895), a warning to cycling enthusiasts! (Below) 'Hygenic' saddle advertised in 1895.

ANATOMICALLY PERFECT

(Below) Singer Tricar (c.1905)
(Right) Century Forecar, 1899.

for these events were enormous in size and totally unsuitable for normal road use. During this period, and before the science of engine design and tuning had been properly developed, the simplest way to increase the speed of an inefficient machine was to increase its size, and therefore the power of the engine.

But speed need not necessarily depend on engine size, and some competitors proved this with properly-designed and well-prepared machines. It was recognized that the large cumbersome machines used for record breaking were freaks. In the United States, although the 'monster' machine had its following, the motorcycle as a practical means of transport got off to a slow start, there being virtually no petrol-engined machines before 1900. In

beginning, and there is no doubt that both played a big part in moulding the American industry. The company which made the Indian motorcycle was formed in 1901 and, alone among its contemporaries, realized at a very early stage the value of a healthy export market. As a result, Indian machines became almost as well known in Britain as in America. Harley-Davidson arrived on the scene a little later. In 1903 William S. Harley teamed up with Arthur Davidson in Milwaukee to produce a little two-h.p. belt-driven machine quite unlike the larger vee-twins which characterized the company's output after 1909.

But these were by no means the only American makers during this period. Throughout the length and breadth of the country hundreds of companies both large and

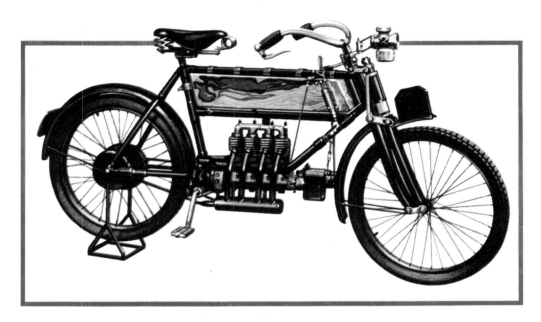

F.N., 1905, a Belgian motorcycle built by Fabrique National d'Arme de Guerre *of Liége, the manufacture of which continued until 1923.*

Biggest bicycle ever built, in the United States in 1896, was the 'Decemptuple', or ten-seater.

comparison with Europe, American roads outside towns and cities were virtually non-existent (a situation which persisted well into the 1920s in some areas) and the motorcycle was at a distinct disadvantage compared with other modes of travel.

The two names which put American motorcycles 'on the map'—Indian and Harley-Davidson—were in at the

small offered a bewildering selection of machines. Some American designs were eccentric but many were advanced for their time. Indian introduced a twist-grip handlebar control as early as 1904, for instance, and from 1913 the Minnesota-built Cyclone offered a vee-twin with overhead camshaft on their production models when other manufacturers were destined to use this only for racing specials.

Indian motorcycle, 1911.

A significant event in 1907 was the first Tourist Trophy race organized by the Auto Cycle Union. Although inter-city road racing was allowed on the Continent, the British government would not permit racing on the public high-way under any circumstances. While this did not prevent a few illegal sprints and trials taking place in outlying districts, a long distance event was out of the question. It was for this reason that the A.C.U. approached the government of the Isle of Man. Fortunately for the industry and the sport they not only gave permission for the closure of 25·6 kilometres (sixteen miles) of roads but also entered enthusiastically into the spirit of the event by agreeing to give limited sponsorship.

From the very earliest days, motorcyclists had been conditioned to accept the fact that although the brand name on the machine they rode with such enthusiasm might be British, French or American, the engine which propelled it was very probably imported from elsewhere. In addition, motorcycle manufacturers were highly export-minded, and the motorcycle itself, because of its relatively small size and the ease with which it could be broken down into component parts for shipment, lent itself to this attitude. The result was a healthy interchange of ideas and competition between the manufacturing nations.

During the bicycle craze in the 'Gay Nineties' in the United States, a popular place for a spin was the Riverside Drive in New York.

The Tourist Trophy Race

The start of the Senior Tourist Trophy Race on the Isle of Man in 1928. The first T.T. race, organized by the Auto Cycle Union, was in 1907. It came about because motorcycling organizations in Britain were worried about the regulations governing the International Cup races held in France since 1903. These placed the sole restriction on entries of an overall weight limit of 50 kilogrammes (108½ pounds), which resulted in competitors squeezing the largest and most powerful engines possible into the flimsiest of frames. These machines were dangerous and unstable and contributed little to the design improvement of ordinary touring machines. The A.C.U.'s formula for the T.T. races was more practical, ruling out freaks and monstrosities, and encouraging the development of machines which were not far removed from those in everyday use by the ordinary motorcyclist.

4 War on Two Wheels

While the First World War (1914–18) is generally accepted as being the first fully mechanized conflict between nations, the idea of using the motorcycle as a weapon of war was by no means new. As mentioned earlier, the Simms tricycle had been fitted with a Maxim machine-gun as early as 1899, and the Cudell was adapted to tow a light cannon in 1900. Apart from these isolated instances, the potential of the motorcycle in numbers was realized at least as early as 1903. In September of that year the Motor Volunteer Corps in Britain was advertising in *The Motorcycle* for members to take part in autumn manoeuvres, as a sort of Territorial unit. Then, in 1905, the newly formed Automobile Association organized the transportation of a brigade of Guards by road to Hastings, in order to demonstrate the part which mechanized transport could play in military affairs. By 1913 this potential had, in many areas, been fully realized. The Indian Army, for instance, could boast a fully operational Motorcycle Corps fitted with machine-gun sidecars, and with special clips on the front forks which were designed to accommodate a rifle.

When the First World War broke out in September 1914 a British Expeditionary Force was speedily assembled to cross the Channel to support the French, and as with any rapidly moving army there was a desperate need to establish and maintain an efficient chain of communication. This is difficult enough at the best of times, but is doubly so in time of war.

Once again, the pages of *The Motorcycle* were the means by which volunteer motorcyclists were recruited, and initially their main role was that of despatch riders. At the outset, there seems to have been no co-ordinated plan of action on the part of the War Office, who spent large sums purchasing huge quantities of second-hand machines which were then impressed into military service. While this may well have been the best and quickest way of getting the despatch riders into action at short notice, difficulties inevitably arose.

Of the riders themselves, there were no complaints. Most of them were keen motorcyclists who had been only too glad to offer their skills to their country in this way. But it must be remembered that by 1914 there were vast numbers and types of machines on the market, most of them admirable in their way, but not all suited to despatch work in the rough conditions they were expected to face. With dozens of different makes in use, the problems of spares and servicing very soon became apparent.

As the business of running the war got under way, the authorities decided to standardize on a few basic types of machine, and to award the manufacturers contracts to produce these for direct delivery to the Army. Of the successful contenders for these contracts, Douglas supplied their flat-twin 2·75-h.p. models and Triumph their four-h.p. belt-driven model H—a direct descendant of their famous 3·5-h.p. model—to the Army, while the Royal Flying Corps favoured the Phelon and Moore (P. and M.) 3·5-h.p. model.

Trade mark of the Aurora Automatic Machinery Company, New York, famous for their six h.p. light twin machine of 1915.

Triumph motorcycle, 1914.

Most of the work was done by the Douglas and the Triumph and huge numbers were built. The choice was a good one, and these machines gave unstinting service under the most arduous conditions throughout the war with little change in their specification. What is more, they gave many soldiers their first taste of motorcycling—Douglas and Triumph motorcycling in particular—the fruits of which were to prove beneficial to both companies once the war was over.

These machines were not usually modified in any particular way for military use, but there were others which had more specific duties to perform. Of these, a number of Nortons (which had proved themselves promising in pre-war competitions) were fitted with ambulance sidecars carrying fitted stretcher and first aid equipment, although more often activities under the protection of the Red Cross were performed by converted private cars, many of which were driven by their owners.

The Motorcycle Machine Gun Corps, on the other hand,

French and British cycle troops pass in review before the Allied Chiefs of Staff.

was equipped with vee-twin sidecar machines, mainly of Clyno or Royal Enfield manufacture, upon which were mounted Vickers machine-guns and ammunition boxes. Angus Scott also designed a peculiar three-wheeled device using his water-cooled two-stroke engine, which also carried a machine-gun mounting, but very few were built following the proving trials. The design was not wasted, however, for when Scott sold his interests in the motorcycle company after the war he used the machine-gun carrier design as the basis for a small three-wheeled car. Other 'heavies' employed by the M.M.G.C. were the Zenith and the Matchless. On the latter the hapless gunner was slung well out over the back of the sidecar on a sprung outrigger. Never really effective, the machine-gun unit was eventually replaced by the armoured car, but quite large numbers were built and not a few—mainly Clynos—found their way to the Russian front.

At this time wireless telegraphy was still in the development stages, and even aircraft had no wireless contact with the ground once they had taken off. By 1918, this state of affairs was being very slowly remedied. Therefore, apart from carrier pigeons—which were widely used by both sides in the war—the main method of communication was by car or motorcycle, and motorcycles could often go where the car could not. This was particularly true in areas of intense shelling, where craters and mud sometimes rendered roads impassable to heavy traffic.

With the entry of the United States into the conflict in 1917, further units of motorcycle machine-guns and despatch riders arrived. These used mainly Indian machines which, while they rendered sterling service, were not as successful as the lighter British machines.

Throughout the war inventors were at work. The Germans introduced an all-enveloping cape fitted with two 'windows', one to enable the rider to see where he was going, and the other to permit the lamp of the machine to shine ahead. It cannot have been very effective for, although it would have provided a welcome measure of protection to the rider in the rain and mud of the battlefields, it would have restricted his movements severely

Colt machine-gun mounted on an army bicycle.

Levis motorcycle, 1916.

Despatch riders were vital for communication in the First World War.

if not completely unseating him. Also, since motorcycle lamps during the period were lit by acetylene gas, the fumes would eventually have asphyxiated him.

No more successful was the tiny mini-bike introduced by Hugo Gibson, an American from New York, the engine of which drove the rear wheel direct. A bracket was provided on one side of the cross-bar on which to clip a rifle, but since the whole machine with its scooter-like wheels was so close to the ground, it would no doubt have sunk without trace in the mud had anyone been foolhardy enough to put it into service.

More ingenious was the Harley-Davidson 'single' adapted by the Americans to be ridden by soldiers who had lost an arm in battle. A metal sleeve was attached to the handlebar into which the artificial limb was inserted, thus giving the rider proper control. This was not the first

Motorcycles in wartime provided mobile ambulance services.

Dursley-Pederson folding bicycle, 1890s.

Rudge 'Multi', 1915.

American machine to be so adapted, however. Before the First World War, Dan Cassidy, a well-known rider who had been a champion board track racer, lost an arm in a hunting accident. He had an eyelet welded to the handlebars of his Indian racer and with a hook in place of his hand continued racing with great success.

Ahead of its time, but far more practical, was the German idea of a transparent windshield with leg fairings to protect the rider. This device, too, never really caught on, although it was to be re-invented some 30 years later and enjoyed considerable popularity.

The German army made wider use of motorcycles than their British counterparts, although they did not employ so many. In addition to despatch work and sidecar machine-gun units they also adapted combinations to run on rails, to act as snow-ploughs and ambulances, and even serve as miniature field kitchens. Towards the end of the war Germany suffered from an acute shortage of rubber and a number of alternatives, including sprung iron tyres, were tried. While these proved reasonably successful on cars and heavy trucks, they were found to be quite unsuitable for the lighter motorcycle.

The Ner-a-Car, 1915.

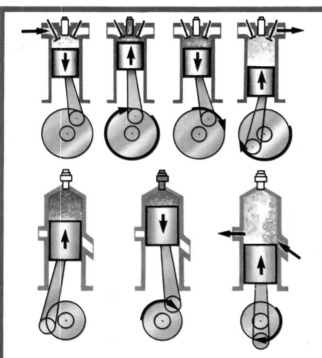

In the four-stroke engine (top) power is produced by four strokes of the piston, but in the two-stroke (above) the power is produced by only two strokes of the piston.

Kickcycle designed in Chicago in 1917.

Sport during the war came virtually to a standstill, although a number of 'all-khaki' races were held at Brooklands until 1915 for members of the armed forces home on leave or awaiting embarkation. The serious business of winning the war took precedence thereafter, and the track saw no further activity until 1920.

During the post-war years there was a tremendous increase in the popularity of motorcycling, both in the Allied countries and in Germany, although for different reasons. The war years had proved a testing time for all the participating countries, and not least for the machines with which the war had been fought. The motorcycle emerged tougher, more practical and reliable than before, and the end of the war signalled the beginning of a new and prosperous era in the industry.

A number of indirect benefits resulted from the war years. Many manufacturers found themselves with enlarged premises, greater production facilities, and healthy bank balances as a result of their lucrative war contracts. During the war it had been found that many tasks in the assembly and manufacture of motorcycles, which traditionally had been carried out by men, were just as efficiently performed by women—at cheaper rates of pay. The labour force available was therefore much larger. Although some years were to pass before the electric lighting sets pioneered by Bosch in Germany, and those of other firms, were to gain universal acceptance, the concentrated effort which had been put into aero-engine technology, particularly in the field of air-cooled engines such as the Gnome and Le Rhone rotaries and radials, produced valuable technical progress which was employed to good effect in motorcycle factories.

There were problems, however. In many cases, the

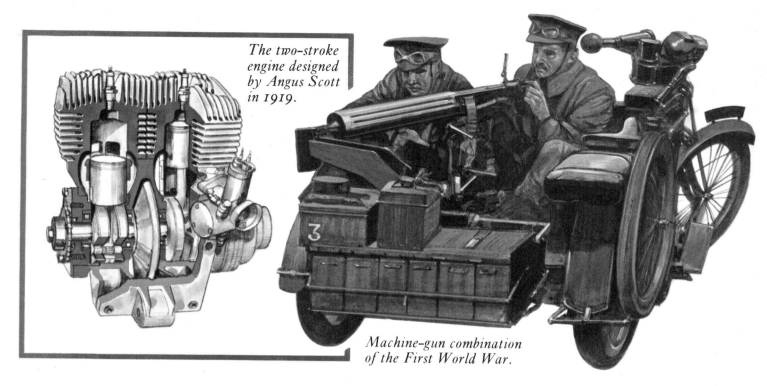

The two-stroke engine designed by Angus Scott in 1919.

Machine-gun combination of the First World War.

Armistice took manufacturers by surprise, and the sudden cessation of hostilities left them with huge and expensive factories and large labour forces with nothing to produce. It was essential to make the transition from the conditions of war to those of peace as soon as possible and to attract new customers. With the armies of the world demobilizing by the thousand this was not difficult. As we have seen, many soldiers had their first experience of motorcycling while in uniform and this naturally encouraged a desire in them to possess their own machines upon return to civilian life. But to supply the new demand was not, at first, as simple as it might have seemed. After the long war, there were chronic shortages of raw materials everywhere. Germany was nearly bankrupt and large areas of France and the Low Countries had been devastated.

There was also the problem of what to do with all the machines that had been supplied for army use, which had survived the battlefield and were now surplus to requirement. For every second-hand ex-military machine which was sold at public auctions, the manufacturers lost the sale of a new machine. In Britain, for example, thousands of ex-military Douglas and Triumph machines flooded the market and could be picked up very cheaply.

Another factor in the fight for sales was the entry of aviation companies into the market. During this end-of-war period there were so many surplus aeroplanes awaiting disposal that the companies found it almost impossible to sell new ones. They therefore turned to the production of motor cars and motorcycles in an effort to remain solvent. Such was their haste to start earning again that many of the designs which came on the market suffered from being too far advanced for general acceptance, and often insufficiently

tested. The established manufacturers who had learned their business the hard way in the pioneer years before the war generally did very well, and although post-war inflation increased prices to something like four times their pre-war level, sales were running at a high peak by the 1920s.

In Germany, motorcycles also enjoyed a boom after the war. During the 1920s something like 500 firms entered the market—must of them manufacturing lightweights. Great industrial concerns, ranging from the huge steel and armaments combine of Krupp to luxury car and airship engine producers such as Maybach, hastily turned to the production of motorcycles in one form or another. Inevitably there was fierce competition and, against the odds, such well known makes as B.M.W. and D.K.W., Mars and Zundapp, all of whom were newcomers during this period, survived to take their place alongside established veterans like N.S.U.

America, too, enjoyed a post-war increase in the popularity of the motorcycle. As before, most favoured were the Excelsior, Indian and Harley-Davidson machines. But the slump of the early twenties almost killed the industry. Car makers like Henry Ford, whose products were already ridiculously cheap, slashed prices by 25% in an endeavour to stimulate sales and this completely knocked the bottom out of the motorcycle market. After all, who was going to buy a motorcycle when he could have a motor car for roughly the same price? Thereafter the largest customers for Indians, Harley-Davidsons, Excelsiors and the few other makes which managed to weather the storm, were the police departments in the various states. The interest of the public centred on motorcycling as a sport, and the touring machine was virtually finished.

31

Wheels and Badges

All vehicles in modern times tend to be streamlined, and this is the result of the scientific study of shapes which will reduce wind resistance, a consideration that did not greatly affect the early designer.

The cycle, and its powered cousin the motorcycle, have arrived at their present-day appearance through the evolution of a bewildering array of shapes. Particularly in the early days of the cycle, many of these shapes appear absurd to us and it is sometimes difficult to guess at the designer's intention in making them. The ordinary, with its enormous front wheel, is an example of this. But it came about because the designer wanted to achieve higher speeds by increasing the diameter of the driving wheel which the rider pedalled. Cycles in the nineteenth century went through practically every possible variation of the single-wheeled monocycle to two-, three- and four-wheelers. By the time the motorcycle took the scene the basic two-wheeled shape had been well established and the principal concern became one of where to put the engine. Today the small wheeled bicycle and the scooter-like motorcycle seem to be logical attempts to provide a convenient mode of transport for modern conditions, although the 'superbike' and the lightweight racing bicycle will continue to command the admiration of the enthusiast.

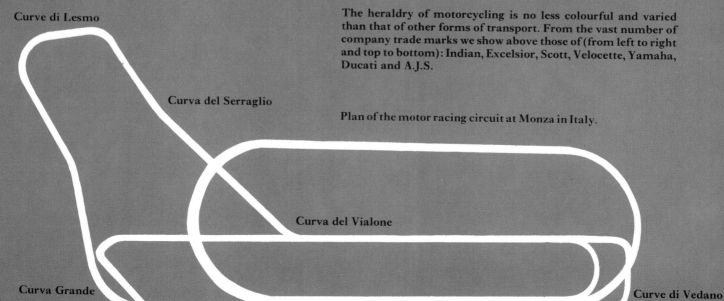

Curve di Lesmo

Curva del Serraglio

Curva del Vialone

Curva Grande

Curve di Vedano

The heraldry of motorcycling is no less colourful and varied than that of other forms of transport. From the vast number of company trade marks we show above those of (from left to right and top to bottom): Indian, Excelsior, Scott, Velocette, Yamaha, Ducati and A.J.S.

Plan of the motor racing circuit at Monza in Italy.

5 The Golden Years

The war years had given to women the freedom to do men's work and the 1920s were a period during which the general emancipation of women progressed steadily. It was natural that some attempt should be made to popularize motorcycling for women. The changing social attitudes made it more acceptable for women to ride motorcycles and the fashion for shorter skirts made it easier for them to do so. One manifestation of the trend was the scooter phenomenon which is dealt with later in the book. As for the motorcycle proper the demand was for a light, fully-enclosed machine with a low centre of gravity and more stability than was normally afforded.

One of the most successful designs, though for a limited period only, was the Ner-a-car, built by Sheffield-Simplex, first in Tinsley, near Sheffield, and later in Kingston-upon-Thames. Designed by an American, J. Neracher of Syracuse, New York, it was built under licence by the Sheffield company, and in retrospect seems a most unusual choice to add to their range. At the time, this English company was better known for their luxury cars (discontinued in 1922) and lorries. In the event, the Ner-a-car attracted few female buyers, although it did spark off a vogue for fully-enclosed machines, of which one of the most notable—although financially unsuccessful—was the Pullin–Groom designed by ex-T.T. rider Cyril Pullin. Like the German Mars, it employed a pressed steel frame rather than the tubular frame of its competitors and (another German idea) a windshield with leg guards. It survived until 1925, and the following year the Ner-a-car bowed out too. Pullin was to try again in 1928 with his Ascot–Pullin, but chose the wrong time to introduce what was a revolutionary design.

During the depression of the early 1930s motorcycle producers were hard hit and many companies went out of business. In the United States, few firms had survived the earlier slump in 1921. Cleveland, one of the few companies to market small two-strokes successfully during the twenties, switched to large four-cylinder machines and cars, but failed in 1929. The Illinois-based Excelsior company, which had always been a poor third in the sales race with Indian and Harley-Davidson, were the only other firm of any importance in the business and enjoyed a loyal but diminishing following of enthusiasts. When they shut down in 1931 they took with them the popular four-cylinder machine designed by William Henderson, and their other makes, the Super-X and the American-X (which was the name given to Excelsior machines exported to England, to avoid confusion with the Birmingham-built machine of the same name). The American motorcycle industry was then effectively reduced to just two names—Indian and Harley-Davidson—and that was the way it remained until the mid-1950s.

Early American inter-city races and track events were enacted largely on dust roads where it was necessary for the riders to develop special skills to deal with the atrocious conditions. Some effort was made to counteract the poor natural surfaces by the provision of closed-circuit wooden board tracks, but these proved dangerous and unpopular with riders. Following several fatalities they were gradually discontinued, except for cycle racing, for which they had originally been designed. For generations horse trotting had been a popular American sport and the closed-circuit horse trotting tracks, surfaced with loose grit, became a popular venue for motorcycle racing events. Techniques which had been perfected on the dust roads were admirably suited to the conditions which these tracks afforded, but because they were circuits it was necessary to evolve methods of rounding the bends continuously without loss of speed or balance.

Colloquially known as 'dirt tracks' they quickly attracted attention, and riders responded by adapting their machines and their techniques of riding to suit them. The method of broadsiding was evolved whereby the rider would fling his machine into the bend amid showers of dirt, steering into the inevitable skid, with the rear wheel broadside to the track and steadying himself by extending his left boot—of tough leather shod in steel—and trailing it like an anchor. By 1913, the one mile record for dirt track racing in America stood at more than 133 kilometres (83 miles) per hour. From Canada and the United States the sport moved to Australia, where horse trotting was also popular, and two leading Australian riders, Billy Galloway and Keith McKay, decided to gamble a season's winnings in an attempt to popularize the sport in England.

The King's Oak public house in Epping Forest, near London, was the chosen venue for the first meeting in February 1928. A 402-metre (440-yard) cinder track had been built and a crowd of 30,000 spectators flocked to watch. Although speeds attained were only about 64 kilometres (40 miles) per hour, the spectacular nature of the riding provided all the excitement the crowd needed. By 1930, upwards of 50 tracks were planned or in operation and by 1936 the sport was sufficiently organized worldwide to warrant the holding of a World Championship event.

B.M.W. supercharged twin-cylinder machine on which Georg Meier won the 1939 Senior T.T. Race.

Georg Meier.

Joe Wright on his A.J.S. before his world speed record attempt at Southport Sands in 1933.

Winners of the Dutch T.T. races of 1933 (from left to right), Ivan Goor, G. de Ridder, Ted Mellors, Piet van Wyngaarden and Stanley Woods.

Tiger Stevenson at West Ham speedway track, London, 1930–1 season.

Mud trials with motorcycle and sidecar in the 1930s.

Despite this early interest in new forms of racing, the general trading outlook in 1930 was depressing. In the motorcycle world a number of firms were hanging on only by the skin of their teeth. They were so weakened financially that they either faded out altogether in the late thirties, or lingered painfully on producing machines which would never compare with those made in the industry's hey-day. New designs and innovations continued, however (designers often seem to operate at their best in conditions of financial stringency), but the most immediate result of the slump was a drastic fall-off in sales, which continued until 1933.

There are a number of reasons why the drop in business was arrested in the case of the motorcycle industry. First and foremost—and probably the reason why so many companies managed to survive—was the simplicity of even the most sophisticated motorcycle when compared with a motor car. Manufacturers soon found ways in which to cut back non-essentials to provide a practical utility machine to sell at a very low price. In this way they were able not only to retain their old customers, but to attract new ones.

In Britain in 1931 the motorcycle press talked of a £12

utility machine for the working classes, and while it is difficult to see how a profit could be made at such a figure, the actual prices charged were not very much more. A 98-c.c. Excelsior cost just £14·75 and the standard utility model could be purchased from a number of makers for between £19·80 and £23. For this you could expect a 148-c.c. two-stroke, usually with a Villiers engine, with full equipment and capable of carrying two people in comfort and complete reliability. In this class firms like Francis-Barnett, Excelsior, Levis, Royal Enfield and Coventry-Eagle were typical,

the economic depression throughout the world.

Because of all this sporting activity, the larger machines did not die. In fact, the thirties spawned some remarkably successful and long-lived designs in the 'heavy' class. Notable among these was the Ariel Square Four or 'Squariel' as it was immediately dubbed. Originally introduced as a 500-c.c. machine when first shown in 1929, it quickly grew up and the capacity was increased to 600 c.c. in 1935 and 1,000 c.c. in 1936. Basically two parallel twins joined together with their flywheels geared to revolve in

Cycle racing in a New York stadium in the 1930s.

Stanley Woods on a 350-c.c. Velocette.

and even Douglas, who had for so long offered little but flat-twins, added to their list a Bantam model with 148-c.c. Villiers two-stroke unit, although the engine was fully enclosed and laid horizontally to give the impression that the traditional layout had been adhered to.

The conventional medium and large machines continued to be made, although in smaller numbers, and competition at both local and international levels continued unabated. One of the side-effects of the high unemployment of the period was that it gave people more time for leisure. Provided, therefore, that public entertainment could be provided cheaply enough it was almost bound to be well attended. During this period, people wanted to forget their troubles and anything which enabled them to do so—even for a few hours a week—was popular. The cinema enjoyed the biggest boom in its history, especially with the coming of the talkies, and motorcycle sport, particularly at amateur level, mushroomed. Club events, which had been gaining in popularity throughout the twenties, flourished everywhere. Competitors and spectators alike had no shortage of trials, rallies, hill climbs, all-night runs, grass track events and mud trials to take their minds off the seriousness of

opposite directions, the Square Four proved remarkably smooth in operation and was very popular for sidecar work. It was a versatile machine, and in supercharged solo trim was capable of lapping Brooklands at 179 kilometres (112 miles) per hour in 1934—with the smaller engine at that. Originally a chain-driven overhead camshaft operated the valve mechanism, but when this was exchanged for pushrods in 1936 the machine was destined to a production life of 22 years with only detailed improvement.

But the Square Four was a gamble, and the cost of tooling up and producing a machine of this type very nearly ruined Ariel. They closed down for a period in 1932 but managed to solve their financial problems and were back in business by the end of the year. Triumph, who were allied to the car company of the same name, were also having a difficult time, despite the fact that they also offered a 147-c.c. lightweight. Their staple offering was the 650-c.c. Page-designed vertical-twin—another large machine—and when the parent company decided they could no longer cover Triumph's losses, they sold out to Ariel. Thereafter the two companies prospered together.

In between the lightweights and the heavy twins and

fours, the medium single-cylinder machines continued with little change to provide the backbone of the industry. Design improvements had increased potential power output but the majority of models, with their larger saddle tanks and accessories, gained in weight too, and this offset any improvements in overall performance. While Scott persevered with their water-cooled two-stroke design with little change, they appealed to a very specialist market and built no low-priced machines. It was left to Germany to really develop the two-stroke principle on larger machines.

Hitler and the Nazis came to power in 1933, largely as a result of the unsettled conditions that followed the depression which had thrown five million Germans out of work. Throughout the thirties, and under Nazi rule, Germany became more and more powerful, and for propaganda reasons sport of all kinds was heavily subsidized by the government. This is not to belittle the achievement of the German engineers, and while Mercedes and Auto-Union were sweeping the board in Grand Prix motor racing, D.K.W. developed a range of two-stroke machines which encompassed everything from lightweights to a 500-c.c. twin. The result of all this development activity was D.K.W.'s success in the 1938 Lightweight T.T. event, when a supercharged 248-c.c. machine won at 125·57 kilometres (78·48 miles) per hour. Always advocates of the flat-twin, B.M.W., unlike Douglas in Britain, favoured a transverse layout. They, too, demonstrated the supremacy of larger German machines by winning the last pre-war Senior T.T. with their supercharged 500-c.c. o.h.c. flat-twin ridden by Georg Meier.

Multi-cylinderism was not confined to Britain, Germany and the United States, and one machine in particular is worthy of note even though it was virtually unknown outside its native Denmark. The countries of Scandinavia have never been foremost among motorcycle producers, and it is therefore all the more remarkable that one of the few machines to emerge from there proved to be one of the

Badges of the
A.A. and R.A.C.
motoring
organizations.

longest-lived, both in terms of production and design. Built in Copenhagen, the Nimbus first saw the light of day in 1920, and with its 750-c.c. air-cooled in-line four-cylinder engine, rear suspension and shaft drive it was a refined machine. Acquiring a pressed steel frame in the thirties, it continued virtually unaltered for 37 years and was a familiar sight on Danish roads in the yellow livery of the Danish Automobile Club until production ceased in 1957.

With the British motoring organizations, the A.A. and the R.A.C., providing one patrol for every twelve miles of road, it might be thought that more women would have taken to two wheels. But apart from the open-framed 'sit-up-and-beg' autocycle which did tempt some district nurses and lady golfers, attempts by the manufacturers to woo the fair sex failed dismally. Prominent among those who tried to popularize a fully-enclosed machine for

*The tandem was popular
for touring in the 1930s.*

*Cyclists rally at Alexandra
Palace near London, 1936.*

universal use, but with a special eye on the lady rider, was Francis-Barnett. With a 250-c.c. two-stroke engine, all enclosed mechanical parts, pressed steel forks and low centre of gravity, their Cruiser looked modern, if somewhat inelegant and received an enthusiastic reception in the motorcycle press. But even such advanced features as the provision of an ignition key failed to tempt buyers. With a top speed limited to 86 kilometres (54 miles) per hour it could never appeal to the real enthusiast, but tired examples were still to be seen in use over twenty years after their introduction, which says much for the merit of the design.

Not that women shunned the sport entirely. Some, like Edith Foley, competed regularly on the continent of Europe. Riding French Peugeot machines, she became a familiar contender in trials and participated in the Paris–Pyrenees trial for the Touring Cup of France. In Germany Ilse Thouret and Thea Haagner took part in some pretty gruelling long distance trials, but these intrepid ladies were very much in the minority.

By this time, T.T. racing had grown to international proportions. Although the Isle of Man event was still considered the premier race, T.Ts. were held in the

Standard safety bicycle of the 1930s.

Sidecar racing, 1938.

Netherlands, Spain and other Continental countries. Such was the enthusiasm for the sport that it was common for parties of enthusiasts—particularly those members of the International Motorcyclists Tour Club—to travel up to 3,200 kilometres (2,000 miles) on their machines in order to attend. Italy, too, emerged as a force to be reckoned with when, in 1935, Moto-Guzzi took part in—and won—the Senior T.T. on the Isle of Man. It was the first time that British supremacy had been successfully challenged in the Senior since U.S. Indian's win in 1911, and the first time a fully sprung machine had won, too. The engine layout was interesting since, although it followed the well-tried vee-twin configuration, the front cylinder was almost horizontal.

Not only did this lower the centre of gravity and, together with the advanced springing, improve the road holding of the machine, it also improved cooling of the rear cylinder, always a problem with vee-twins.

It was now becoming clear that British manufacturers were lagging behind in the field of technical innovation and that their products were beginning to look dated. Typical of the new breed of machines from the Continent was the Puch vee-four two-stroke. The design represented all that was good in the modern application of the two-stroke principle and its compact good looks contrasted favourably with the vertical single four-stroke which was still the mainstay of the British market.

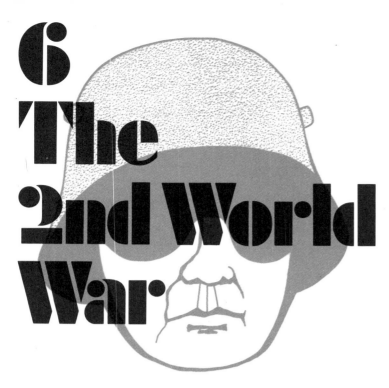

6 The 2nd World War

So far as Britain was concerned, the first eight months of the Second World War were a little unreal. The comparative inactivity provided a breathing space which the country badly needed, but in many ways it led people into a feeling of false security. Apart from the organization of defences and air raid shelters, and the setting up of the Home Guard and all its ancilliary services, life appeared to go on much as usual.

This may have been how it seemed to the general public, but the military authorities certainly made good use of the time. All the indications in the late thirties had pointed to a conflict sooner or later, and after the lessons of the First World War, over 20,000 motorcycles were already in service on the day war was declared. An Army Motorcycling Board of Control had been set up to train riders, and with the advances in technology in the years between the wars, the industry was in an ideal position to supply as many machines as would be required. Once again, *The Motorcycle* played its part in the recruitment of volunteers

Variable speed gears of various types have been used on cycles since the 1870s. Dursley-Pederson bicycles used a three-speed hub gear in 1902, the same year in which schoolmaster Henry Sturmey and engineer James Archer patented their form of three-speed hub gear. Large numbers of these were made by the Raleigh Cycle Company, and together with the subsequent four-speed gear (1938) Sturmey-Archers were to become the most famous cycle speed gears of all. They had free wheel in all gear ratios and (a later development) a trigger control for gear changing mounted on the handlebars, which replaced the older and less convenient type of lever mounted on the top frame tube.

to serve as despatch riders. The imposition of petrol rationing effectively curtailed the activities of civilian motorcyclists. There was a good deal of squabbling over petrol allocations, and riders of small machines such as autocycles successfully campaigned for the introduction of 0·5-unit petrol coupons because their tanks would not hold a full gallon of fuel.

Despite the fact that most of the established manufacturers were awarded contracts to supply the Army with machines, large firms like Ariel were still producing their full range for home consumption, and the smaller companies like Scott and Levis were advertising 'business as usual'. This situation was to continue until 1940 in some instances. By that time shortages of essential materials, fuel restrictions and a diminishing home demand, coupled with the channelling of all engineering facilities into the war effort, ensured that home production dwindled away. As was to be expected, with so many men enlisting in the services, a glut of used machines came on to the market, and by late 1939 Pride and Clarke—one of the largest dealers in London—were advertising machines for as little as £5 'to ride away'.

Many people continued to believe that the war would not last long, and advertisements at the beginning of 1940 were still talking optimistically about 'when we return to normal conditions'. Six years were to pass before that situation was achieved. Fuel restrictions led to speculation about alternatives to petrol, but the most practical outcome of rationing was renewed interest in the extreme lightweight or autocycle. Francis-Barnett introduced their 98-c.c. Powerbike, which looked remarkably like its predecessors of 30 years earlier, even to the provision of pedals. With a top speed of about 48 kilometres (30 miles) per hour, it certainly did not break any new records, except that of its exceptionally low fuel consumption which produced 56 kilometres per litre (158 miles per gallon).

While the experience of war often speeds up the advance of technology, particularly in the aircraft and motor car industries, in some ways it has been responsible for a retrograde attitude so far as motorcycles are concerned. Of the machines supplied by the major producers, B.S.A., Matchless, Royal Enfield, Triumph, Ariel and Norton, the majority complied with the Army requirement for large side valve singles of 350–500 c.c. Apart from a few overhead valve machines which happened to be already in production when the war broke out and which were impressed into service, the side valve type, renowned for its reliability, simplicity, ease of servicing and slogging characteristics, was perhaps the obvious choice. To satisfy the Army, a number of companies who had for long concentrated on the more advanced types, turned their research departments once again to the question of improving side valve design.

Against this background, Italy—still not at war—was going ahead with her 1940 racing programme and concentrating on advanced machines with supercharged four-cylinder engines, like the Bianchi, Benelli and Gilera.

The 500-c.c. Gilera, perhaps the fastest road racing machine in Europe, developed 90 b.h.p. at 8,000 revs per minute, while the Benelli was a model of compactness with its water-cooled transverse-mounted four of only 250 c.c., complete with twin gear-driven overhead camshafts. The Bianchi favoured air-cooling and its twin overhead camshafts were shaft-driven.

In the main, the British machines were simply successful civilian models devoid of trimmings and painted in matt khaki, whereas those supplied to the German Army tended to be purpose-built for military service. It must be remembered that the initial German victories in the war were accomplished by means of blitzkrieg tactics. That is to say, by the rapid advance of troops and armoured divisions into enemy territory, with artillery and air support, and the avoidance of long drawn out and expensive battles where both sides were 'dug in', as in the First World War. In order to achieve this rapid mobility it was necessary to rely on a highly mechanized Army, and motorcycle units became the logical successors to the cavalry regiments of old. Typical of the machines evolved for this type of warfare was the N.S.U. Kettenrad, a sort of cross between a motorcycle and a light tank.

Steered by a single front wheel and handlebars, the Kettenrad was a mini-halftrack powered by a 1·4-litre four-cylinder Opel car engine mounted in a central position. It could accommodate three passengers at a squeeze (all facing rearwards) in addition to the driver. It had the advantage that it could negotiate very rough terrain at speed, and being semi-enclosed was not so badly affected by water when called upon to negotiate boggy ground or shallow streams and rivers. First employed effectively in Crete, it was later deployed in large numbers with Rommel's Afrika Korps in the Western Desert, where hundreds were captured by the Allies after the fall of El Alamein. That battle being decisive, however, little use could be found for the strange machines in the Allied armies, and almost without exception they were scrapped.

Airborne troops in the Second World War were sometimes equipped with miniature motorcycles which were landed by parachute with the men.

The United States entered the war after the Japanese attack on Pearl Harbor in 1941. By then large numbers of Indians and Harley-Davidsons were already in use in the American Army, both as solos (fitted with a clamp for a rifle on the front forks and ammunition box panniers) and combinations. Some of these American units were still referred to as 'cavalry'. As the war progressed, however, the Jeep became more popular and replaced the combination in most theatres of war.

German infantry mounted on cycles enter a Belgian town.

Prominently featured in early German films and news-reels of the war, conventional sidecar units were also extensively used in blitzkreig tactics. These machines were almost exclusively the province of B.M.W. and Zundapp. Many were built with a driven sidecar wheel from a solid rear axle, and this accounts for the spectacular way in which the front wheel left the ground when the machines were accelerated violently from rest.

Captured examples of the B.M.W. were extensively copied by the Russians as their M.72. In addition to use with the Red Army they were also produced after the war in civilian form well into the 1960s. The Russians were not, of course, the only ones to find captured machines useful. When the Germans occupied the Channel Islands, they made considerable use of the large 1,000-c.c. shaft-driven F.N. type M.12 combinations which they had captured from the Belgian Army.

Most sidecars used with the B.M.W. and Zundapp machines were of the standardized Einheits type, suitably adapted to carry machine-guns or mortars. Later in the war some of their duties were taken over by the Volkswagen Kübelwagen, a four-wheeled slab-sided general purpose vehicle similar to the Jeep, which also appeared in amphibious form. Solo machines were generally 250-c.c. N.S.U's. D.K.W. two-strokes and German Triumphs, the latter having originally been connected with the British Triumph firm until they went their separate ways after 1929.

Japan's military contribution to the motorcycle scene gave no indication of the influence she was later to exert in peacetime. Like most of the other vehicles in use in the Japanese Army, motorcycles were strongly influenced by American design. Like the German machines, they were largely standardized, and while principally built by Kurogane and Sankyo were modelled on the Harley-Davidson. Most of Japan's pre-war vehicle assembly plants were laid out on American lines and set up with American technical assistance. General Motors had an assembly plant of their own in Japan, which was taken over by Toyota.

These then were the principal machines in use by the combatants, although large numbers of machines which never saw a battlefront were pressed into service for war work of one type or another, particularly in Britain. In Manchester a battery of OK Supremes was fitted with shielded rearward-facing lights to pilot buses and trams through the city during the blackout, a necessary precaution imposed while Germany was inflicting heavy damage with night bomber raids. For the same reason, all headlamps on motorcycles and other vehicles in Britain were cowled to prevent their being seen from the air.

With the setting up of munitions factories away from city centres, where they would have been obvious bombing targets, the problem of transporting workers from their homes to factories was largely solved by encouraging them to use light autocycles, and by providing special petrol allowances. Fuel was still a problem and was to continue to be so, but the owner who advertized his Vincent-HRD for sale in 1940 with the comment 'will run on paraffin' was probably being over-optimistic. There was even talk of reintroducing steam as a motive power for two-wheelers, although this did not meet with much enthusiasm. While the majority of car owners either sold their vehicles at give-away prices or laid them up 'for the duration', motor-cycling in one form or another gained a growing band of

Vincent motorcycles were the highlights of the 1954 Motorcycle Show in London.

The main parts of a motorcycle.

1. Piston. 2. Air cooling fins. 3. Connecting rod. 4. Crankcase. 5. Exhaust valve. 6. Exhaust pipe. 7. Main crankshaft bearing. 8. Magneto. 9. Carburettor. 10. Petrol tank. 11. Petrol filler. 12. Oil tank. 13. Oil filler. 14. Footrest. 15. Gearbox. 16. Kick starter. 17. Foot change gear lever. 18. Toolbox. 19. Silencer. 20. Driving chain and sprocket. 21. Rear mudguard. 22. Front fork spring. 23. Steering head. 24. Twist grip throttle control. 25. Brake lever. 26. Head lamp. 27. Front mudguard. 28. Saddle. 29. Tyre valve. 30. Knee grip.

A stunt rider on the 'Wall of Death', a popular spectacle at fairgrounds.

followers and in March 1940 there were no less than 37 makes of lightweight offered at prices ranging from £20 to £34. Predictably, and as had happened during the First World War, women took over the work of men and were even employed as despatch riders in the armed forces.

By 1941, the larger machines such as the A.J.S. and 16H Norton were no longer available new to the buying public, and even advertisements for lightweights had begun to disappear. Acute paper shortages meant that the motorcycle press—in common with all other magazines—had to choose between publishing monthly instead of weekly or cutting out most of the advertisement pages, and they decided on the latter course.

Norton also experimented with sidecar units equipped with a driven sidecar wheel in 1941, but this type was never adopted by the Allies to any great extent. As the situation in

Europe became more confused, and Britain acted as a refuge for the remnants of the fighting forces of countries which had fallen to Germany, a strange assortment of machines and nationalities came to be seen on British roads—Czechs on Terrot combinations, Free French and Poles on Indians and even a Russian on a B.S.A. Countless volunteer civilian organizations were set up to augment the police and the military and among these the University Civil Defence Despatch Riders, manned by enthusiastic undergraduates, performed sterling work.

The bicycle, too, became an essential tool of the war machine, and quite apart from the valuable part it played in the fuel-starved civilian communities, it was developed for direct military use. In particular the United States Airborne Infantry were equipped with folding bicycles, which could be dropped with the infantry by parachute. After landing, the machine was unfolded and a couple of wing nuts tightened, then the soldier was completely mobile within seconds. This theme was developed still further with James and Royal Enfield producing 98- and 125-c.c. lightweights (called 'flying fleas' by the troops) to be dropped with parachute regiments. The Research Centre at Welwyn Garden City, Hertfordshire also produced the Welbyke with a 98-c.c. Spryt engine and 12·5-in. wheels. Collapsible, it was small enough to be strapped to a soldier's back, and in a tight spot was just capable of transporting two men to safety. It was later produced in peacetime as the Corgi by Brockhouse Engineering of Southport. America also developed the airborne bicycle to its logical conclusion with the Cushman 53, a scooter of even more spartan appearance than the Welbyke but developing greater power from its single-cylinder engine. It was also designed as a tricycle and for use with a sidecar, but never gained much favour in wartime, although, like the Corgi, its peacetime

The Vintage Motorcycle Club was founded in 1946 when 38 riders attended a formative meeting in Surrey. At first, the club limited membership to owners of pre-1931 motorcycles and three-wheel cycle-cars but, as the years have passed, this has been extended to include all machines over 25 years old. The current membership of the club, which is spread all over the world, tops 4,000. The club came about to combine the interests of those enthusiasts who were proud possessors of pioneer machines, and to seek out and preserve examples of early motorcycles which might otherwise have landed on the scrapheap. Some of the vehicles which turn out regularly for trial runs include a 1924 Ner-a-Car, a 1904 Humber tri-car, a 1916 Harley-Davidson and, in the 1898 Werner with engine in the steering-head of the frame, the oldest motor bicycle still able to take to the road under its own power.

successors were popular as runabouts and with golfers.

In 1943, Britain's *Manchester Guardian* was generous in its praise of the quality of German motorcycles used in the Tunisian campaign. According to its special correspondent, 'their motorcycle, for instance, were beautiful jobs, far superior to ours'. Although the remark was not well received, praise for enemy machines continued in the British press. Despatch riders who had served in the Western Desert and ridden captured Italian and German machines were critical of the rigid-framed British machines. Some indication of the problems which were being experienced with supplies of raw materials and spares may be gained from reports that in India Harley-Davidsons were being repaired with captured D.K.W. and Bianchi spares.

By late 1943 suggested designs for post-war machines were already being discussed, and these ranged from diesel machines to motorcycle kits for home assembly. Strange to relate, motorcycle sport never completely died out during the war. Enthusiasts carefully hoarded their petrol allocation and a trickle of trials and grass track events continued to be reported at amateur level, although there were no events of any great significance. Under the guise of training courses— which indeed they were—semi-sporting events, to which spectators were invited, were also held by those organizations who had both the fuel allocation and the justification for staging them. These were the forerunners of the auto-cross events in which service riders take part to this day. So the wartime scene was not entirely without interest.

Prototype Scott motorcycle, 1946/7.

German motorcycle combination equipped with machine-gun.

Facts & Figures

GEOFF DUKE

English racing champion, Geoff Duke, who started the great days of his sporting career riding Nortons, switched to the Italian Gilera in 1953. One of Duke's most important contributions to motorcycle racing was the design of special lightweight clothing which cut down weight and wind resistance, and improved speed. Duke won the 500-c.c. world championship four times, once on a Norton and three times for Gilera.

LIGHTWEIGHTS

With the improvement in roads, the establishment of a network of competent garages and motorcycle shops, and the general increase in the popularity of motorcycling, there arose the need for a light machine, suitable for the younger rider, simple to maintain and economical to operate, but capable of covering quite long distances if required to do so. It is difficult to say who produced the first really practical machine of this category, but foremost in the field and certainly one of the best in the world was the Levis. Introduced in 1911 as a 211-c.c. two-stroke, it was hailed as a pioneer and by 1914 its reputation was firmly established. America too produced a crop of short-lived lightweight designs but generally the machines were of heavier construction than most of their European counterparts.

MONSTER BIKES

This giant motorcycle, built in 1937, was powered by a special Plymouth six-cylinder car engine. It had three speeds, an electric starter, and steering was by remote control with a chain from the handle bars to the steering head. Such monster motorcycles in the United States were dubbed 'racing monstrosities' and received a great deal of adverse comment from those people who were more sensibly concerned with improving efficiency and reliability than in recording speeds which would have been dangerous—indeed, impossible—under normal road conditions.

BARRY SHEENE

Still in his teens, Barry Sheene, a member of the Suzuki team, represents the new generation of motorcycling superstars, and together with Phil Read (M.V. Agusta) and John Williams (Yamaha) is once again proving that British riders can be among the world beaters in international motorcycle sport. Surviving a terrible crash in practice at Indianapolis, he was racing again within three months, after many had predicted that his career was finished, and in July 1975—a mere twelve months or so since the disaster—he clocked up a Formula 750 Championship win and a World Championship 500-c.c. win in Sweden, riding in heatwave conditions and setting new lap records in both classes.

GEORGE BROUGH

The 'Rolls-Royce' of the two-wheeled world was the Brough Superior. George Brough was to motorcycles what Henry Royce was to cars—a perfectionist. Born into a motorcycling family— his father had been building machines of various types at Basford, Nottingham since 1908—he wanted to build a machine to excel all others but was unable to persuade his father to back his ambitions. Undaunted, he set up his own works in 1921, unashamedly calling his new machine the Brough Superior. From the outset, Brough products were built regardless of cost and although initially the machines were merely assembled from bought-up parts, these were invariably built specially by outside firms to Brough's specification and design. His dedication was soon rewarded, and when in 1923 the first J.A.P. vee-twin powered models were replaced by the SS 80 Speed model, he had the satisfaction of seeing it lap Brooklands at over 160 kilometres (100 miles) per hour, the first side-valve machine ever to do so. It was followed by over 50 outright wins in succession, and when his improved SS 100 o.h.v. was introduced in 1924 it was sold with a 160-kilometre (100-mile)-an-hour guarantee. Adoption of Castle sliding-action front forks gave vastly improved handling and steering, and through the medium of these beautifully finished machines, and the Alpine Grand Sport, Pendine and Black Alpine which followed them, the Brough Superior had, by the end of the decade, built up a devoted following bordering upon religious mania.

WANKEL ENGINE

The Dutch Van-Veen rotor OCR 1000 is right into the superbike class. The engine, developed by Van-Veen from the Comotor Wankel, produces 100 b.h.p. at 6,500 r.p.m. and has a maximum speed of 240 kilometres (150 miles) per hour. It has a 4-speed gearbox, hydraulic dry clutch and shaft drive. The cooling system is described as water integrated with oil. Again smoothness and low noise level is claimed as one of the major characteristics. Van-Veen says that they chose a Wankel engine as the power unit for their new super bike because the power, size and weight ratios were the best available, and because of its lack of vibration and noise at high speeds.

BARAGWANATH AND LE VACK

No book on motorcycles would be complete without mention of E.C.E. Baragwanath (above), an Englishman despite his unusual name. Favouring large machines usually with sidecar attached, he first came to prominence riding his o.h.v. vee-twin Zenith. By the mid-twenties he had graduated to a Brough Superior and it was on this that he became a legend on the track. When he later acquired a supercharged Brough Superior outfit he became unbeatable. Bert le Vack (right) was another outstanding rider/tuner—a titan of the inter-war racing scene. He is best known for riding on Indian machines, the first of which, an ancient 1911 eight-valve vee-twin, was nicknamed 'the Camel'. By April 1921, and with valves made of special steel, Le Vack was able to coax the Camel up to 170·4 kilometres (106·52 miles) per hour, just one day too late to qualify for the title of the first motorcycle to exceed 160 kilometres (100 miles) an hour at Brooklands, although in 1922 he did become the first to lap the track at over that speed.

RACING IN AMERICA

The Indian Motorcycle Company, like the American Excelsior (not to be confused with the British company of the same name) and, by 1916, Harley-Davidson too, had cut their teeth in the rough and tumble of America's half-mile and mile dirt tracks, and in the gruelling city-to-city races of up to 480 kilometres (300 miles), the County Fair events and on the wooden banked board tracks. In many cases the rules were conspicuous by their absence, the competition fierce, especially where prize money was involved, and the going was rough. To survive, let alone win, it was necessary for every member of a team to be on his toes and contribute to the fullest extent in his own way. It was probably due as much to team work of the highest calibre, as to the merit of the machines and the skill of the riders, that the Indian team were so successful in the 1911 Tourist Trophy race. Certainly they taught the other contenders a thing or two about pit work. After 1918 there was no shortage of sporting activity, with mountain and hill climbs and cross country marathons, as well as track racing.

J.A.P. ENGINES

The year 1903 was something of a milestone in the history of motorcycling, for it was then that J.A. Prestwich first offered their range of engines to manufacturers and, although they were not the first company in the field, the impact of J.A.P. engines was destined to be felt in every country of the world which manufactured motorcycles and their influence was to last for over 30 years.

GLENN CURTISS

In 1907 at Ormond Beach, Daytona, American pioneer airman Glenn Curtiss is said to have reached the incredible speed of 219 kilometres (137 miles) per hour on a motorcycle fitted with a 40 h.p. V-8 air-cooled aeroplane engine. Curtiss piloted this monster over four miles, two to achieve the speed, one to maintain it, and one in which to slow down and stop.

UNO-WHEEL

Walter Nilsson's Uno-Wheel was produced in 1936 after ten years of experiment to develop a motor-driven single wheel. Powered by a single-cyclinder twelve h.p. motor, speeds of up to 160 kilometres (100 miles) per hour were claimed for this machine. Steering is accomplished by a device which allows the rider to remain upright while the wheel leans in turning.

GLOSSARY OF TERMS

Belt drive System whereby power from engine is transmitted to driven road wheel by means of a belt.

Combustion chamber Area above piston in cylinder into which fuel mixture is compressed and ignited.

Combination Motorcycle fitted with sidecar attachment.

Diamond frame Arrangement of motorcycle frame tubes into roughly diamond shaped area.

Horizontally opposed twin Engine having two cylinders arranged at 180 degrees to one another, either longitudinally in the frame or transversely.

In-line twin Engine having its two cylinders arranged one behind the other.

Knee grips Rubber pads fitted to the side of petrol tank.

Motor wheel Arrangement wherein engine was contained within spokes and around hub of the driven wheel itself.

Overhead valves Arrangement—normally conducive to enhanced performance of engine—whereby valves are built into 'ceiling' of combustion chamber.

Saddle tank Name given to petrol tanks which straddle cross-bar of machine.

Shaft drive System which transmits drive to rear hub by means of revolving shaft and bevel gearing.

Side slip Meaning simply to skid sideways.

Side valves Arrangement whereby inlet and exhaust valves of an engine exist side by side on 'floor' of combustion chamber.

Sociable Early name given to sidecar attachment.

Square four Two vertical twins, 'Siamesed' together with flywheels geared to revolve in opposite directions.

Supercharger Device whereby fuel is pumped under pressure into combustion chamber.

Vee-twin engine Engine with two cylinders arranged in vee formation longitudinally in frame of machine.

Vertical twin Normally engine with twin cylinders cast integrally side by side and mounted transversely in frame.

7 The Scooter Story

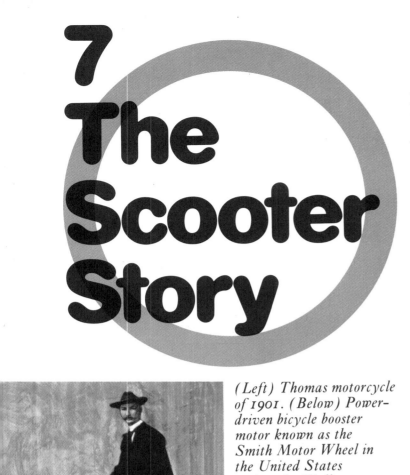

(Left) Thomas motorcycle of 1901. (Below) Power-driven bicycle booster motor known as the Smith Motor Wheel in the United States and as the Wall Autowheel in Britain.

Fashion in vehicle design, as in all things, comes and goes, and apart from the lightweight motorcycle, there has been no more persistent contender for favour than the motor scooter. What is more, it seems to have gained in popularity with every appearance.

The first machine to adopt the scooter layout was probably made by the British firm of Singer in 1903. It used a Perks and Birch motor-wheel in front as motive power, with a flat platform slung low to the ground behind it, supported by the rear wheel, and upon which the rider stood upright. Singer were a company full of bright ideas for developing their motor-wheel, and this is just one of several layouts which did not progress very far. Two years later, in 1905, a more serious attempt was made by the sponsors of the Brown Midget Bicar which, in addition to its armoured wooden frame, carried weather-guarding reminiscent of that to be seen on modern machines. It made little impression, however, any more than did a later design, the bucket-seated Italian Laviosa, although bucket seats did enjoy a brief revival (in America in particular) in the period 1912–15.

The year 1912 saw the introduction of the remarkably advanced-looking machine called the Swan. With its all-enclosed bodywork of pressed aluminium and the absence of a cross-bar, it looked extraordinarily like machines which were not to appear until after the First World War. Built in Warrington, Lancashire, it had faded into obscurity by 1913.

The motor-wheel concept was again introduced in 1910, this time by A.W. Wall of Birmingham, a very inventive and unorthodox engineer. The Wall motor-wheel powered not only a stand-up-to-ride scooter of the simplest front-

wheel drive design, but an array of devices from powered ice skates to five-wheeled motor cars and railroad inspection trolleys, all of diminutive size. Wall also built a shaft-driven scooter at about the same time, but while his motor-wheel was still to be seen in America until the late 1920s, the scooter did not survive.

The absence of lasting success in any of these early designs makes it all the more difficult to understand exactly what happened in 1919 once the First World War was over: it can only be described as a scooter 'explosion'. Literally dozens of makes appeared on the market overnight, of all shapes and sizes and varying degrees of simplicity and quality. It is perhaps an over-simplification to say that this was solely due to the need for cheap transport in the immediate post-war years. There was more to it than that. In the first place, being so simple, the scooter could be put into production very quickly, without the installation of expensive plant and tools. For this reason

Heinkel Tourist
motor scooter, 1960.

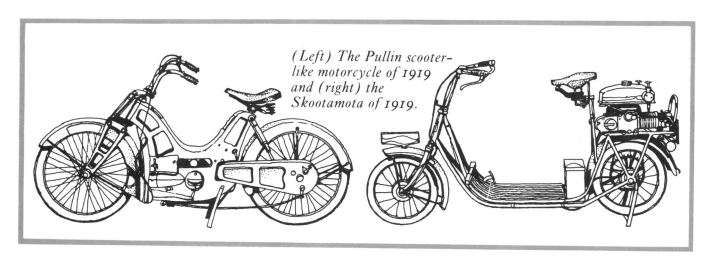

(Left) The Pullin scooter-like motorcycle of 1919 and (right) the Skootamota of 1919.

it was a popular choice with the aircraft makers who, as we have seen, faced a lean time when their war contracts ended. Among such aircraft firms were Sopwith Aviation (in conjunction with A.B.C.) who produced the Skootamota, another Granville Bradshaw design, and the Gloucester Aircraft Company with their Unibus. This was a really well designed and substantial machine with fully enclosed mechanics, a pressed steel chassis on car lines with leaf springs for the front and rear wheel and a 269-c.c. two-stroke engine larger than most on the market.

The Avro Monocar, designed by Sir Alliot Verdon-Roe, one of the pioneers of flight, was perhaps the most sophisticated scooter of them all. Again fully enclosed, it owed more to car design than to the motorcycle, and had a car-type seat, dashboard with windscreen, coil springs with shock absorbers and electric lighting. Steering was by means of a T-shaped joy-stick, obviously borrowed from the Avro aircraft.

At the other end of the scale was the Kingsbury, a design of the stand-up-to-ride variety, consisting of little more than a single-speed mobile platform. Many other manufacturers offered this type. Apart from the advantages to them of being quick and easy to build, there were two main reasons for their popularity. The first was their appeal to women. The increased freedom which women had gained during the war, when they had done everything from driving ambulances and working in munitions factories to being 'clippies' on the buses, had led many of them to show an interest in owning their own means of transport. The scooter was designed for them. Children's nannies were even catered for by Dunkleys, the pram manufacturer, who offered the Pramotor, a combined pram-cum-scooter in which baby sat up front in a conventional pram-type carriage (some enclosed with windows) while nurse stood on a little platform at the rear in front of the engine and steered the contraption.

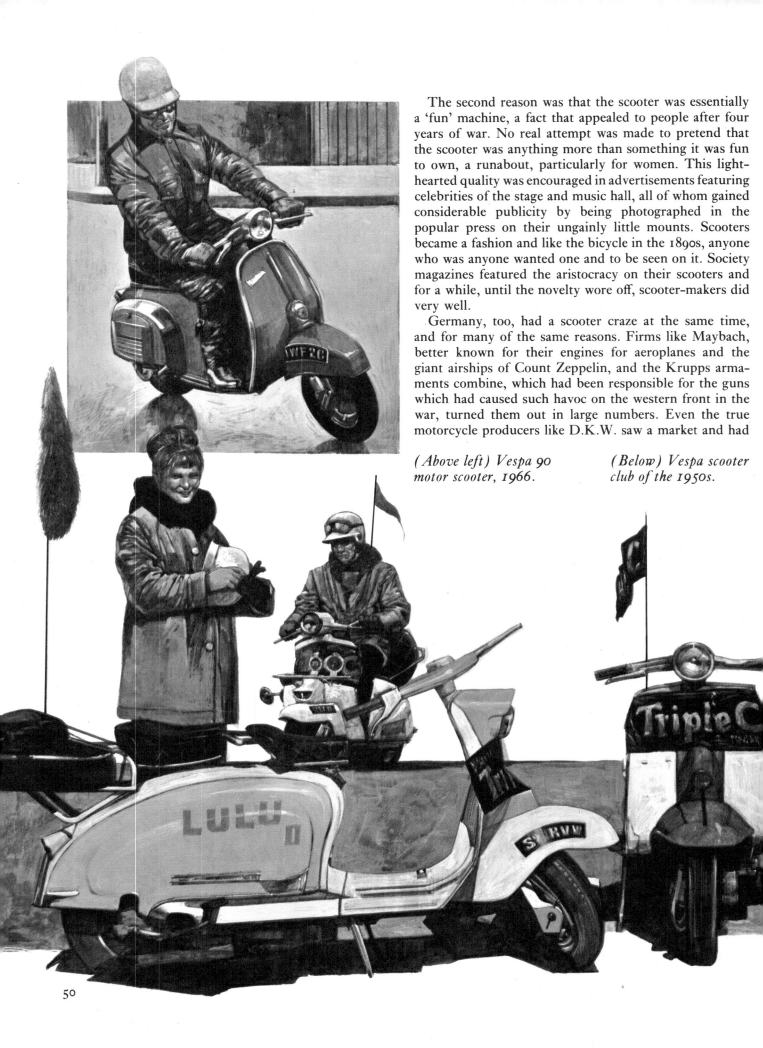

The second reason was that the scooter was essentially a 'fun' machine, a fact that appealed to people after four years of war. No real attempt was made to pretend that the scooter was anything more than something it was fun to own, a runabout, particularly for women. This light-hearted quality was encouraged in advertisements featuring celebrities of the stage and music hall, all of whom gained considerable publicity by being photographed in the popular press on their ungainly little mounts. Scooters became a fashion and like the bicycle in the 1890s, anyone who was anyone wanted one and to be seen on it. Society magazines featured the aristocracy on their scooters and for a while, until the novelty wore off, scooter-makers did very well.

Germany, too, had a scooter craze at the same time, and for many of the same reasons. Firms like Maybach, better known for their engines for aeroplanes and the giant airships of Count Zeppelin, and the Krupps armaments combine, which had been responsible for the guns which had caused such havoc on the western front in the war, turned them out in large numbers. Even the true motorcycle producers like D.K.W. saw a market and had

(Above left) Vespa 90 motor scooter, 1966.

(Below) Vespa scooter club of the 1950s.

*Modern racing bicycle with the Moulton
small-wheel bicycle in the foreground.*

great success with their rear-engined Golem. But it couldn't last, of course, and when the first post-war slump occurred in 1921 and everyone was brought back to reality with a bump, one of the first casualties was the scooter. America had been scarcely affected by the craze, only the Autoped making any impression, and elsewhere it had caused little interest compared with that in Britain and Germany. The scooter disappeared almost as quickly as it had appeared. The aviation companies who produced them either went out of business or returned to making aeroplanes, motor cars or other products, and the true motorcycle firms concentrated on conventional light-weights at the lower end of their range.

And so the situation remained for virtually twenty years. The late 1930s saw the appearance of a few crude machines of the scooter type in America, but these were mainly designed for use on golf courses or to be sold by big department stores as 'super toys' to the children of the wealthy. It was not until 1941 that a really worthwhile and modern-looking machine appeared, and this was an Anglo-American product. Built by Johnson Motors of Los Angeles, it utilized Villiers three-speed engine-gear units of 125 c.c. and 196 c.c., and with its small diameter front and rear wheels enclosed in 'spats' and large balloon tyres it looked remarkably modern. With the world at war it was doomed to failure, and the only successful scooter types to be produced during the period were the military Cushman and Welbyke, already discussed.

When the war ended there was no scramble for scooters, unlike the period which had followed the First World War. Apart from the Swallow Gadabout, a rather boxy tubular-framed machine built by the Swallow sidecar

company's offshoot in 1948, the scooter was a vehicle conspicuous by its absence.

When the scooter 'invasion' did come to Europe, in 1949, it began in Italy in the form of the Vespa (Wasp). Designed by the Italian Piaggio aircraft company and built by them from 1946, it was made in Britain under licence by Douglas and very quickly its popularity spread. It was also built in Germany and France under licence, and almost before anyone realized it the whole of Europe was scooter crazy again. Italy, having initiated the revival, benefited most, and in 1951 her population of motor-cycles suddenly quadrupled to nearly half a million. That figure was doubled in 1952 and by 1953 was up to 1·75 million—and all because of the scooter. Not only this, Italy was exporting scooters as fast as she could make them, and by 1954 they accounted for practically 70 per cent of the total value of cars, motorcycles and lorries produced by the Italians.

Innocenti of Milan also commenced exporting their Lambretta machines, which differed from the Vespas in that they were shaft-driven. These two types of scooter became the most popular of all, with Vespa and Lambretta clubs springing up all over Britain and on the Continent.

With such a phenomenal success story, other manu-facturers were bound to try and capture some of the market. Numerous makers launched their own scooter designs, some of them, like Puch, Zundapp, Durkopp, N.S.U. and D.K.W., motorcycle manufacturers of long standing. Others, like Dayton and Dunkley, were drawn from the ranks of cycle and pram manufacturers, or like Heinkel, from the aircraft and heavy vehicle industries. B.S.A. also built a scooter for which they resurrected the

As far back as the 1890s the idea of simply adding a light petrol engine to an ordinary bicycle to provide motive power was common enough. Since the beginning of the century engineers had experimented with motor-assisted bicycles. Commercial motorized cycles after 1900 developed along two lines. The first of these led to a machine still based on the bicycle, but specially built around the engine attachment on the steering head. The other was the standard safety bicycle to which a cyclemotor was added in such a way that the structure of the machine remained unaltered. These cyclemotors were the true ancestors of the modern units such as the British Cyclemaster, the 35-c.c. B.S.A. 'Winged Wheel' unit and the Hercules rotary-engine unit. All these types and others on the continent of Europe evolved after the Second World War, when considerations of economy revived the demand for a cheap form of mechanical transport.

(Right) Mobylette Cady.

(Above) Velosolex 5000.

(Right) Honda Amigo.

(Below right) Peugeot V.R.

famous Sunbeam name. But the result was hardly worthy of the name, and it was the last machine to wear the golden sun badge. Watsonian, the famous sidecar makers, produced a mini-sidecar for scooter use, called the Bambini. The Netherlands, never a prominent producer, introduced the Sachs-engined Bitri, and France the Manurhin Hobby (under D.K.W. licence). Others well known at the time were the Italian Rumi Ant and the English Wolverhampton-built D.K.R.

Alongside this scooter revival was a general swing away from heavy machines, and a whole crop of strange devices appeared. Heading a rearguard action against the scooter invasion, makers of the older type of open-framed auto cycle like Bown, Raynal and New Hudson were suddenly faced with a new threat—this time from Germany—in the shape of the moped. N.S.U. with their streamlined 49-c.c. quickly virtually swept the board, and they in turn were followed by Leopard, Cucciolo and a whole army of Continental makes.

The 'clip-on' bicycle engine was back in force, too.

There was the Power Pak which, mounted behind a bicycle saddle and driving the rear wheel by friction direct on to the tyre could produce undue wear on the tyre before many miles had been covered. Another was the Cyclaid, also rear-mounted, which reverted to belt drive. Built by the once famous aero-engine and motor car firm of British Salmson, its tiny 31-c.c. engine meant a correspondingly slight aid to cycling! The Cymota favoured the front handlebar mounting position which had been a feature of the first Werner types at the end of the nineteenth century, and incorporated the luxury of a front headlamp in the engine cowling. Vincent, better known for their 1,000-c.c. vee-twin superbikes, also tried to enter the market with their Firefly, which again was driven by friction on the tyre, from a 49-c.c. engine slung horizontally in a central position below the pedals. None of these clip-on designs was very successful, and the only two to achieve anything like lasting popularity reverted to the motor-wheel concept, with the engine mounted integrally within the spokes of the rear wheel; they were the B.S.A. Winged Wheel and the Cyclemaster.

War-torn Japan was also rebuilding her economy. Because of American influence and aid following her victory in the war of the Pacific the few motorcycles and scooters Japan did export in the early fifties found their way mainly to the United States. By 1965, however, the Japanese motorcycle industry was a force to be reckoned with, and a large number of factories, some of them originally in ship-building, textiles and heavy engineering, were turning out competitively-priced machines. Japanese

scooters never made an impact in Europe but large numbers were sold in America during the early and mid-sixties. Prominent was the Fuji Rabbit, a 90-c.c. machine with electric starter, twelve-volt electrics and large motor-cycle-type wheels, but it competed not only with the Vespa and the Lambretta, but with several homegrown examples, including the Harley-Davidson Topper.

While the post-war scooter was primarily a road-going pleasure machine, it was totally unsuitable for competition or cross-country work, and yet indirectly it was responsible for the growth of both. So different was the scooter to the orthodox motorcycle that it bred a completely different type of rider. Being all-enclosed and light to handle the scooter at last became acceptable transport for women, and the necessity of struggling in and out of heavy leather and oilskin clothing was largely removed by the wide protective leg apron and 'floor'. But more important, it encouraged on to the road those who wished to ride purely for fun; it was a light-hearted sociable machine upon which to enjoy oneself.

And so, little by little, the utilitarian role which the motorcycle had earned for itself in wartime faded away, and was replaced by one which provided leisure and sport. Since the scooter was limited in its ability to satisfy the sporting aspect it was gradually replaced by a new type of machine—the high performance, sophisticated lightweight from Japan and, later, Italy. With growing affluence, and the introduction of mini-cars in 1959, riders gradually defected to four wheels, and the scooter craze was—once again—over.

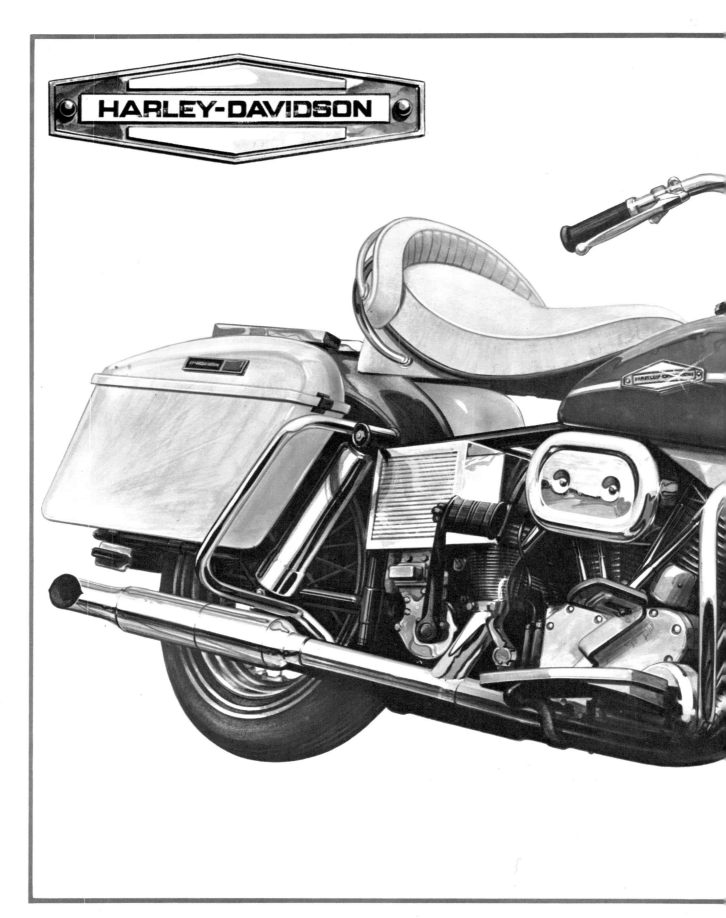

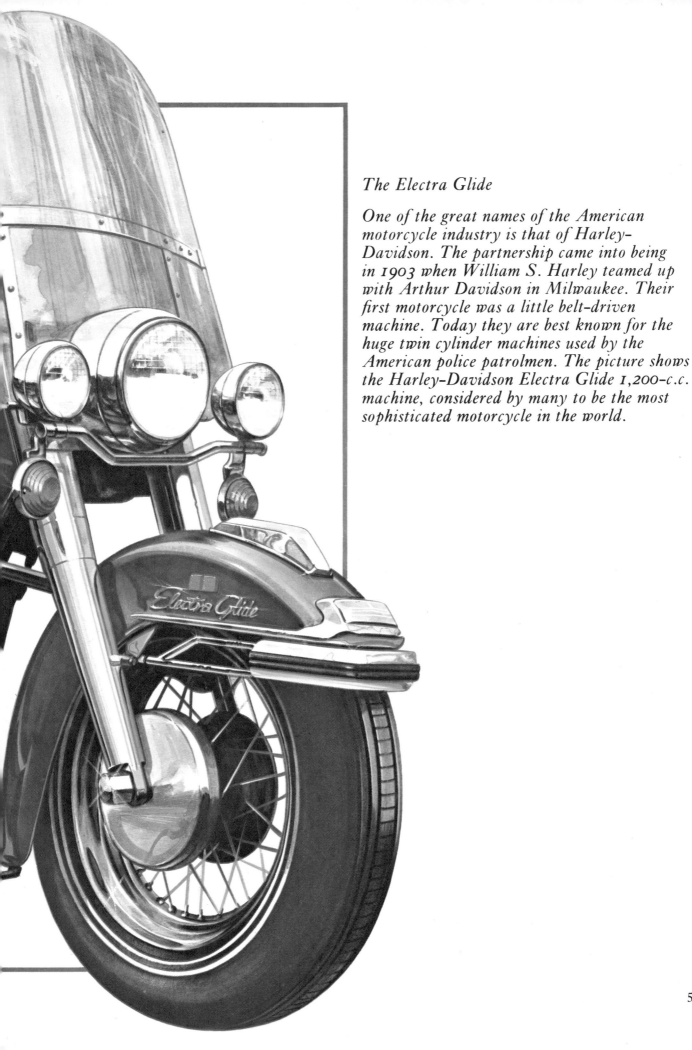

The Electra Glide

One of the great names of the American motorcycle industry is that of Harley-Davidson. The partnership came into being in 1903 when William S. Harley teamed up with Arthur Davidson in Milwaukee. Their first motorcycle was a little belt-driven machine. Today they are best known for the huge twin cylinder machines used by the American police patrolmen. The picture shows the Harley-Davidson Electra Glide 1,200-c.c. machine, considered by many to be the most sophisticated motorcycle in the world.

8 The Modern Scene

The Second World War had left most European countries bomb-torn, short of food and money and with insufficient raw materials for industry. In a way, the immediate post-war years were an extension of wartime conditions without the wartime spirit of national pride and necessary self-sacrifice to make them acceptable. Food was strictly rationed, so was petrol, furniture, clothing and practically all the essentials of life.

Large numbers of government surplus motorcycles were offered for sale to the public, but that was not so damaging to manufacturers as might have been expected. Because of the continuing fuel restrictions many people who tradition-ally had driven cars, turned to two wheels for economy and to make the most of their meagre ration of petrol. New cars were almost impossible to obtain except on the black market, and second-hand cars were fetching very high prices, because most of the few new cars that were being built by the industrial nations were for export. So there was no shortage of customers for motorcycles, both new and

second-hand, and for a while there was a seller's market.

Even by 1949, when the position had eased a little, economy and lightweight machines were of prime con-sideration. Nevertheless, those who had been deprived of motorcycle sport for so long were still prepared to pay good money for a really top class machine. In Britain, the Brough Superior was no more, but its place was taken by the designs of another maker who, although well known in pre-war days, was destined to produce his most renowned machines during the period up to 1956. The maker's name was Vincent and his range of 998-c.c. vee-twins with top speeds of between 192 and 250 kilometres (120 and 160 miles) per hour were formidable motorcycles. The Rapide, priced at £474, was followed by the classics Black Prince, Black Knight and Black Shadow, but despite the fact that these three machines were hailed as the highlights of the Motorcycle Show in 1954, production ceased just two years later. They were the last of the great pre-war vee-twin machines.

But very few people could afford a Vincent, and among the most popular lightweights was the B.S.A. Bantam, a 125-c.c. rigid frame of pre-war looks and performance, favoured by the Post Office for their messenger boys. B.S.A. gave Sunbeam a last fling in 1946 with their S.7., a 500-c.c. in-line twin designed by Ealing Poppe. With shaft drive and fully sprung frame, it was one of the best looking post-war offerings but because of its price it attracted few customers and had disappeared by the mid-fifties.

Douglas stuck doggedly to their flat-twin layout, although they adopted a transverse layout, possibly influenced by the wartime German B.M.W. Last of the line was the Dragonfly, built between 1954–6. By then, Bruce Douglas had lost control of his company which, with a licence to build Vespas in its pocket, concentrated all its production on scooters. The Douglas name, together with the excellent and almost indestructible Dragonfly, was dropped.

Although the British police maintained their allegiance

(Left) Gilera B.500.
(Above) Motobi Sport Special 250.

Modern motorcycle racing combination and (below) the last nail-biting moments waiting for a race to start.

30sec

to B.S.A. in some areas and for patrol duties, their 'maid of all work' was an interesting design from the Velocette stable, and a complete breakaway from the K.T.T. o.h.c. racing model of pre-war days. Designated the L.E., it featured a fully-enclosed scooter-like pressed steel frame which concealed a transverse water-cooled twin of 200-c.c. With shaft drive coupled to water cooling, it was exceptionally quiet and smooth and earned the nickname 'Noddy bike'.

Italy, whose pre-war and wartime machines had been so advanced, tended to concentrate on the transverse four they had previously favoured. In fact, with the Italians, engine development at first took precedence over frame and suspension design. When their machines raced at the Isle of Man T.T., although faster than the British machines, they were outhandled by the Norton 'Featherbed' frame designed by the Irish McCandless brothers (and so called because rider Harold Daniell said riding one was like being on a feather bed). Featuring a full Duplex cradle frame layout with rear suspension by hydraulically-damped swinging forks, it won the Senior T.T. in 1950 at 147·63 kilometres (92·27 miles) per hour in the hands of Geoff Duke, one of the outstanding post-war riders. He subsequently transferred to the Gilera team and thereafter Italian machines ridden by him took the World Championship in 1953, 1954 and 1955. No doubt, Duke took with him his own ideas about frame design learned while with Norton, and these, allied to Gilera's powerful engines, proved an invincible combination throughout the mid-fifties.

In America, Indian, now without the army contracts which had no doubt enabled them to survive during the war years, went out of business and were bought by British Brockhouse Engineering (makers of the Corgi). One of the reasons for the demise of Indian in America was the inroad made into the market by the English Triumph. With their 650-c.c. Trophy, Tiger, Thunderbird and Bonneville (named after the Bonneville Flats in the United States), Triumph continued the successful vertical twin pioneered by Edward Turner in their 1937 range. These large machines not only gained in popularity in America, but sparked off a spate of vertical-twin designs (even in the two-stroke category) in Britain.

By the early sixties, however, the established motorcycle companies in Britain were in trouble. The scooter invasion from Italy and elsewhere had begun, and although most makers were forced eventually to develop scooters of their own, many of them left it too late and only Douglas had any lasting success. Engine design of the medium-to-large machines tended to lag behind that of the Italians, and the more sales that were lost, the less money there was to spend on development and research. By the time it was realized that the scooter 'fad' was to be more than a five minute wonder, time and money were both fast running out. Even Norton, until such a short time before a world beater in the hands of Geoff Duke, were in dire straits in 1962, and only purchase by Associated Motor Cycles avoided collapse.

58

The pace of the race hots up as the leaders jostle for position.

The latter company developed into a kind of mutual protection society for motorcycle firms and eventually encompassed the Villiers and J.A.P. engine companies.

But there were other problems facing the motorcyclist. After the war, insurance companies (who had had a lean time with motor insurance throughout the war) decided to increase motorcycle insurance rates drastically. Motorcycle dealers reacted by forming a Dealers' Union which was underwritten by Lloyds of London and the crisis was averted. By the mid-fifties, with the advent of rock 'n' roll and 'Teddy' boys, the motorcycle again had a very poor image with insurance companies, who frowned on the 'ton up' boys who nightly roared up and down the Great North Road in west London. It became more and more

customers, manufacturers continued to offer the same types as before. With all the big names under the umbrella of Associated Motor Cycles, and all the smaller ones like Dot, Royal Enfield, Velocette and Panther (the latter still producing their forward-sloping 'single' which followed the pattern of their first design for Humber in 1901) unable to do much about it, the British industry was in a very vulnerable position.

Foreign competitors were quick to take advantage of the situation, and outstanding among them was Honda of Japan. Soichiro Honda had no history of shipbuilding or heavy industry behind him. An unsuccessful manufacturer of piston rings, he started his company in a tin shed on a bomb site in Tokyo in 1948. By the early 1960s the com-

(Above) Motorcycle stars of the modern scene (top, from left to right): John Surtees (Britain), Jarno Saarinen (Finland), Klaus Enders (Germany) and (above) Giacomo Agostini (Italy). The scene on the far right above shows the Tour de France cycle race.

Evel Knievel, the American dare-devil motorcyclist.

difficult for young riders with larger machines to obtain full insurance cover and sales dropped heavily. Then the British Government introduced legislation preventing the sale of machines other than those of less than 250 c.c. to learner riders. Instead of rising to this challenge to improve the performance of their smaller machines and win back

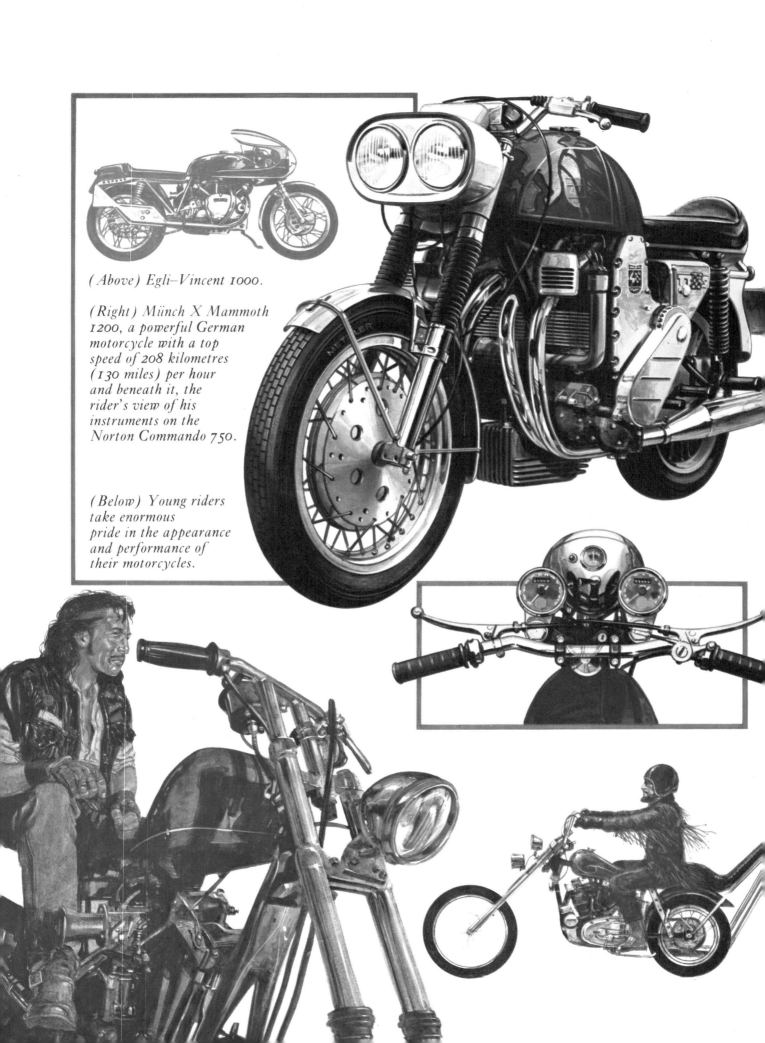

(Above) Egli–Vincent 1000.

(Right) Münch X Mammoth 1200, a powerful German motorcycle with a top speed of 208 kilometres (130 miles) per hour and beneath it, the rider's view of his instruments on the Norton Commando 750.

(Below) Young riders take enormous pride in the appearance and performance of their motorcycles.

pany was the largest producer of machines in Japan and the 'invasion' of Britain commenced.

Contenting himself at first with machines in the utility bracket, Honda quickly captured the moped market with an attractively styled 50-c.c. mount and followed this with the C.B. 72 Sports. Of only 250 c.c. it featured a backbone frame, good looks and the refinement of electric starting. Capable of 144 kilometres (90 miles) per hour, it topped its nearest British rival by 32 kilometres (twenty miles) per hour, and this brought scepticism from those who thought that at such speeds it could last only a few months before 'blowing up'. A few were purchased by A.M.C. and rigorously tested and stripped down. They were found to be built with the precision of a watch. Within a year or so, they outsold all other British makes combined, and captured the American market, too—the last outpost for Britain's dwindling export sales.

The result was inevitable. A.M.C., outdated and badly in need of rationalization, nearly collapsed. Although subsequently reorganized and streamlined, this came too late to save the company. What was left was purchased by Manganese Bronze and reformed as Norton-Villiers. Under new management, Norton survived and by 1967 had re-entered the superbike market with their 750-c.c. vertical-twin Commando.

Ariel, once noted for their large machines, carried on under B.S.A. parentage and finally suffered the indignity of having their name applied to an unsuccessful house-wife's runabout. B.S.A. themselves and Triumph (who had by then amalgamated) lost their American sales, and even a revised range of twin- and triple-cylinder models failed to solve their problems. Ten years after A.M.C. closed down, Manganese Bronze took over B.S.A.–Triumph too.

Of 40 British manufacturers who had been in business in the late fifties, only ten remained in 1972, and of these Velocette were also to go. Scott maintained only a token production, as a sideline to a large jig-and-tool manufacturer who had taken them over; Greeves catered for the specialist moto-cross and mud-plugging competition market; and others made little difference to the overall production figures.

Having almost eliminated the competition, Japan launched a further attack on the superbike market, in which makers like Yamaha, Suzuki and Kawasaki were soon making their mark. By the early seventies, all four Japanese companies were offering a range of machines which covered everything from moped to models capable of well over 160 kilometres (100 miles) per hour. These were augmented by the Bridgestone G.T.R. 350, a new venture by Japan's largest tyre manufacturer in 1970.

The Italians, too, showed that small size was no handicap to performance, and when the scooter market failed they started to produce lightweights which had the advantage of looking anything but what they really were. Sporting styling was their most striking feature, with dropped handlebars, bulbous racing-type fuel tanks and even five- and six-speed gearboxes. They spread their influence to the American market. The Clymer-built Indians had Italian-styled frames, and Harley-Davidson acquired an interest in the Aermacchi company.

Spain, never previously prominent in motorcycle production, also came to the fore with the Bultaco range. This company combined resources with a British new-comer, Rickman, to produce a high performance 250-c.c. two-stroke for moto-cross and trials. Rickman themselves, having commenced with 'one off' specials, went on to supply the police with Zundapp-engined replacements for the Noddy Velocette. In this they share the same combination of distinctions with Greeves, who originally made a name for themselves with police machines as well as scrambles bikes. Greeves, who have always concentrated on the market they know best and thus avoided the problems which beset the bigger companies, are now among the largest producers in Britain.

Norton-Villiers have revived the A.J.S. marque name for off-road machines, and Royal-Enfield (albeit built in Madras in the old Enfield India works) came back into business with a 175-c.c. two-stroke police trainer. Although the names Brough Superior and Vincent are gone, the traditions for which they stood are upheld by the Italian Gilera and M.V.–Agusta and the Japanese Honda, Kawasaki and Yamaha. Following interest by the Mazda

The two-stroke engine is returning to popularity with motorcycle manufacturers today because of study and scientific development carried out by the German and Japanese industries. One of the merits of the two-stroke as opposed to the four-stroke engine has always been that because the oil is mixed with the petrol, lubrication is more or less automatic while the machine is in operation. Now that modern research has enabled refinements to be introduced into the two-stroke its use has been revived in sporting machines up to 250 c.c.

motor car company in Japan in the Wankel rotary engine, Yamaha introduced a Wankel-engined water-cooled five-speed motorcycle—the R.Z. 201 at the 1972 Tokyo Show —and the later recruits in this field, the D.K.W. W.2000 Hercules, the 500-c.c. Suzuki RE-5 shown at the Cologne Motorcycle Show, and the Dutch Van-Veen 1,000-c.c. Comotor-engined 100-b.h.p. water-cooled superbike are exciting machines.

Overall, the motorcycle industry is as healthy as ever it was, proving its adaptability to changing times, particularly with the modern craze for 'chopper' bikes, and there seems no reason why it should not continue to develop and contribute to the leisure and pleasure of future generations.

Index